# TREASURES OF HAVERING
### Listed and historic buildings in
### Romford, Hornchurch, Upminster,
### Rainham, Gidea Park, Harold Hill,
### Harold Wood, Collier Row, Noak Hill,
### Wennington, Cranham and Great Warley

## John Drury

Ian Henry Publications

0 86025 487 9

Published by
Ian Henry Publications, Ltd.
20 Park Drive, Romford, Essex RM1 4LH
and printed by
Redwood Books,
Kennet Way, Trowbridge, Wiltshire BA14 8RN

# CONTENTS

# PREFACE

As a number of you may know, I have put pen to paper before and, following my effort on *The History of Upminster and Cranham* and also the work I did on *Domesday Havering*, I have found it difficult to find a subject of general interest for this third venture into local history. I wanted to write again about the London Borough of Havering, notwithstanding that I now live in Felsted, but with the work that has been done during the last few years there is not much that has not been investigated and written about by one person or another. During the last ten years Ted Ballard's *Our Old Romford and District* has been published and Brian Evans has produced a number of books of photographs and drawings covering Romford and also Hornchurch and Upminster. There have been articles in the local newspapers and what with further articles in the magazines of the Romford and Hornchurch Historical Societies, it seems that not a stone has been left unturned in the delving into the history of the Borough.

The history of an area is made up of people and their properties and consequently I thought it would be a good idea to bring together all the historic buildings of Havering, both past and present, and flavour each entry with some information about the occupants. I have tried to provide a photograph or drawing of each building featured, as it is always better to show a picture, rather than let the reader guess what it looked like. This work is not a complete history of every old building in Havering, down to describing how many bedrooms and bathrooms there were, although some of this information is included in some cases to show the size of the house. Similarly every occupier is not named, but I have picked out the owners where there is a story which I feel would be of interest. The object of this work is to give a flavour of what the properties looked like and snippets of their life from building to demolition, if it is no more. Readers will note that the buildings are not featured in strict alphabetical order, as I have tried to arrange the layout so that a building covering two pages, for example, is seen without turning the page.

I have tried to cover every notable historical property in the Borough and apologise if there is one that interests you that I have omitted. Since putting pen to paper a small area to the east of the borough has been transferred to the Borough of Brentwood and consequently a few properties featured are no longer part of the London Borough of Havering. I would like to thank all those people who have allowed me to photograph their properties.

JOHN DRURY
Felsted, 1998

Bedfords

Upper Bedfords

Upper Bedfords
Parsonage Farm Dairies

# BEDFORDS and UPPER BEDFORDS

These two manor houses comprised the majority of the land between Broxhill Road in the north and east, to Lower Bedfords Road in the south and across to the Bower House in Orange Tree Hill. Nothing is known about previous houses on the sites, until John Heaton rebuilt both properties in 1771. Bedfords was demolished in 1959, although Upper Bedfords is still standing and in use as a private house. Although properties stood on both sites prior to the 15th century, nothing is known about them until they came into the possession of Sir Thomas Cooke of Gidea Hall in about 1460. Cooke held the properties not as freehold but from the Crown as part of the Havering Palace estate. The 'rent' was one red rose to be rendered yearly at the feast of St John the Baptist. The Cooke family held the properties for two hundred years with tenants farming the land and, during this period, the two farms comprised 230 acres.

Lady Ann Sydenham, a member of the Cooke family, owned the estates during the Civil War, but had the properties confiscated by order of Parliament, as her husband was fighting for the Royalists. This ended the long association of that family with the two estates and the farms moved into separate ownership, until John Heaton brought them together again one hundred years later, rebuilding both houses.

Upper Bedfords was also called Earls and the 1771 house was built in a crenallated style with the house looking more like a castle than a farmhouse, although it is said that the property was often mistaken for a church. Bedfords was rebuilt at the same time as a two storey brick mansion with cement rendering. It was altered and enlarged about one hundred years later, with the photograph showing how it looked before demolition. Whilst, on the one hand, John Heaton improved the southern part of Havering-atte-Bower by creating work in his rebuilding projects and the large farming estate he developed, he did cause a certain amount of aggravation in the community by his land enclosures.

Following John Heaton's death the properties passed through various hands until in 1870 coming into the possession of the Stone family, who founded the department store in the Market Place, now Debenhams. The house and grounds of Bedfords were bought by Romford Council in 1933 and used as a museum and public park until the 1939/45 War when the house was occupied by the National Fire Service. The house was empty for many years in the 1950s and, following damage by vandals, it was demolished in 1959. The photograph of the dairy dated about 1907 is a puzzle. It seems to be the Upper Bedfords branch of Parsonage Farm dairy, later known as Risebridge farm.

# BERWICK MANOR

The present Berwick manor house, in Berwick Pond Road, dates from the 17th century, although there have been many alterations and additions since. The house was described in 1769 as a mansion house with visible remains of a larger house. It appears that this property was once a lodge house to a much older manor house, possibly on a different site.

Berwick manor dates from the Domesday Book of 1086 and it seems that, through the centuries, the manor house may have stood on various sites around Berwick ponds. *The Victoria History of Essex* records that the earlier manor houses were probably located north of the present house, although in the 15th and 16th centuries the Hospitallers had their mansion south of the ponds. The Knights Templar held the manor in the 13th century and possibly earlier. This order was suppressed in 1308 and the manor reverted to the king. The manor was then transferred to the Hospitallers who kept it until 1540, when they were also dissolved. The house was demolished in about 1575 after the Dissolution, with only an avenue of trees remaining leading north from the Upminster Road. It is interesting to note that these two important semi-military orders, created in the Crusades, who were devoted to the care of the sick and the pilgrims, should both have possessed Berwick Manor. When Henry VIII dissolved the monasteries the manor passed to Sir Robert Southwell, Master of the Rolls, who already possessed large estates in the area.

By 1710 the Berwick estate comprised 1546 acres (about 3 square miles) with sale particulars in 1729 showing that £32,000 was paid for the lordships of Berwick, Rainham and Moor Hall. This means that the estate stretched from the White Hart public house in Hacton Lane in the north to Rainham village in the south and from Moor Hall farm on the Aveley border in the east to the open land of the Ingrebourne valley to the west of Berwick manor. Like most large estates it was eventually broken up and sold off in lots. Within the original estate there were two lodges, North Lodge, later known as Rainham Lodge, and South Lodge or Berwick House, which assumed the title of Berwick manor, though it is now known as the Berwick Manor Country Club.

Rainham Lodge was quite a large house, having three floors and five bays per floor. It was built in the 17th century and was demolished in 1960. A new house has been built on the same site, but the entrance pillars and railings of the old house remain today. Berwick House dates from the 17th century, with its construction being timber framed. Rendering and recent modernisations have not left it reflecting its true age.

Berwick Manor
Rainham Lodge, Berwick Pond Road

# BOWER HOUSE

The Bower House, previously Mounthavering, is on the east side of Orange Tree Hill, Havering-atte-Bower, and was built in 1729. The building is commemorated by a tablet in Latin in the entrance hall which says:- From the remains of the Royal Palace of Havering Bower, situated on the summit of the hill, this dwelling was founded by John Baynes, Serjeant-at-Law, so that he might retire into sure ease and have pleasure for himself and his friends. A.D.1729.

The wings of the house, as seen in the top old photograph from the rear, were not added until about 1800. The lower photograph is from the front as seen today. The plaque also mentions the name of the architect and the designer - H Flitcroft and C Bridgman - with Sir James Thornhill, who was a painter of murals, being responsible for the decoration of the stairwell which was painted directly on to the walls. The paintings are still there, but unfortunately now behind panelling.

The building covers three floors, with the servants quarters on the upper floor. The house was not particularly large, bearing in in mind the notable people connected with its design and construction. The ground floor comprised a large hall leading from the entrance with four sitting rooms and a study. On the first floor were four bedrooms and two dressing rooms. The basement contained the usual combination of kitchens, wine cellars, etc. The addition of the wings do not appear to have been for any specific purpose other than to create a further dining room and a drawing room. The East Wing contains a fireplace, dated 1659, which was 70 years before the house was built. Although materials for the construction of Bower House came from the site of Havering Palace, it is unlikely that this was the source of the fireplace, as it is known that the Palace site was a heap of ruins as early as 1650. The photographs show a brick building, but earlier records indicate that at one time the house was stucco rendered, with this being removed about 1870.

Bower House does not appear to have been built on the site of a previous property and we are fortunate that the original construction remains today. Unlike many of the notable houses in the Borough, no single family resided there for successive generations and the property was eventually purchased by the Ford Motor Company in 1959 as a training centre. Credit is due to this organisation for the restoration work that they undertook and the centre officially opened on the 16th June, 1960.

The Bower House, rear
Stable Block, Bower House

## BRETONS

Bretons is in Rainham Road, at the south end of the parish of Hornchurch. C T Perfect hardly mentions it in his history of Hornchurch, published in 1917, and it does seem that, due to the house's rather remote location, it was not a popular property with the gentry of the past. It is probable that there was a house here in the 15th century, although there is a reference to a Radulphus Briton in 1177, which could date the estate even earlier.

In 1476, the then owner, Thomas Scargill, made a bequest in his will of ten marks for the building of a steeple at Hornchurch church, although it was not built immediately, as the church was going through a period of rebuilding at this time and the new tower and Scargill's spire were not completed until 1491-2. Without the spire St Andrews would look very much like other Essex churches and thus we have this Breton's benefactor to thank for the distinctive appearance of the church, which can be seen for miles around.

Bretons then passed to the Ayloffe family and it was during their ownership that an Elizabethan house was built. In the late 17th century John Hopkins once again rebuilt Bretons, using some of the bricks and materials from the Tudor house. It was built in the Palladian style. It is said that Hopkins was a miser and known locally as Vulture Hopkins. Although he may have been a miser in life this was made up for by his funeral, which was a very grand affair and one wonders if Hopkins would have approved. Maybe his relations were getting their own back. The poet Alexander Pope wrote about the funeral saying; "When Hopkins dies a thousand lights attend the wretch, who living, saved a candle's end."

The house has retained much of its original features, including the original staircase. In addition to the house itself being a Listed Building, there are two brick barns and a garden wall which are also of significant historic value to be Listed. The older of the two barns has 16th century brick walls.

After the death of John Hopkins, who also owned Redden Court, Harold Wood, the farm passed to John Dare and the property remained in that family's ownership until it was sold to the Romford Local Board in 1869 for use as a sewage farm. In 1976 the sewerage farm was no longer required and the property and much land was bought by Havering L.B.C. for leisure and amenity purposes.

8

# BREWERIES

Local residents are familiar with the Romford brewery site in the centre of the town, recently demolished, but many would be surprised to know that Hornchurch Brewery was established in 1789, ten years earlier than its Romford counterpart. Romford lasted longer though, only closing in 1994, with Hornchurch shutting in 1925 and the buildings demolished in 1930/31.

HORNCHURCH BREWERY stood in Church Hill, now called High Street, on a large site almost opposite the King's Head public house, having a frontage of nearly 100 metres to the High Street and extending back about 50 metres. The site extended all the way to Wykeham Cottage, originally called Rames Cottages, which were leased to the brewery.

The brewery was founded by John Woodfine, with the business remaining in the family for three generations, until sold to Henry Holmes in 1874. Little is known about the original brewing house, but the whole brewery was rebuilt by the second generation in 1838. Thomas Woodfine lived at Brewery House, part of the brewery complex. The third generation of Woodfines got involved in a breach of promise legal case which obtained much publicity locally when Thomas Woodfine called off a marriage to Miss Margaret Smith, who worked in the brewery audit office. The verdict was in favour of Miss Smith, with damages of £3,000: a lot of money in 1856. Thomas Woodfine subsequently married someone else, who bore him seven children. In 1874 at the age of 49, Thomas sold the brewery and moved into farming, first at Dury Falls and then at Lea Gardens, both farms being in Wingletye Lane.

When the Holmes brothers bought the brewery they also acquired various freehold and leasehold public houses, numbering about 36 in total, which included the King's Head across the road, together with the Bridge House, the Cherry Tree, the Crown, the Prince Albert and many more, all within a few miles radius of the brewery. In addition, a further dozen or so pubs, which were not owned by the brewery, were supplied with beer. The brewery expanded in the Holmes period, introducing the manufacture of aerated water and becoming spirit merchants. The business was on the point of being wound up in 1892, when the company was reformed under the title Old Hornchurch Brewery, with the Conron family coming on to the scene. Before lorries transported the beer, the brewery owned 30 horses, which were housed in stables behind the brewery and grazed in a meadow behind the King's Head, to pull the drays. In 1923 the brewery took over Fielder's Brewery of Brentwood. At its peak there were about 60 people employed at Hornchurch, making it the principal employer in the early 20th century. The brewery and the public houses it owned were sold to Mann Crosssman in 1925 and it seems that this forerunner of a large brewery chain was only interested in acquiring the public houses, which numbered about 100 after the Fielder's take-over, as the brewery itself was closed in the same year as purchase. The buildings remained empty until 1930 when demolition was started. All that remains today is a high wall at the back of the block of shops opposite the King's Head, which was the rear wall of the brewery. The old postcard of the High Street is a view looking down from the church with the brewery buildings on the left, which came right up to the road, and the King's Head public house on the right hand side.

Hornchurch Brewery on left; King's Head on right in distance

ROMFORD BREWERY was started in the Star public house in the High Street near the river Rom where beer was brewed in the cellar. The inn was purchased in 1799 by Edward Inn, who was from a farming and brewing family in Baldock, Hertfordshire. The popularity of the beer brewed at the Star, which was bought by other local inns, meant that Edward Inn had to enlarge his brewery from the cellar to larger premises in his backyard. In 1845 he was joined by the Coope brothers and the business became known as Ind Coope. In 1856 a second brewery was acquired at Burton-on-Trent, which was famous for the purity of the water drawn from below the area. The next major merger was with the Allsopp brewery business in 1934, with many more mergers and take-overs since, culminating in the Romford Brewery Company Limited as part of Allied Breweries (UK) Ltd in 1961 and then a division of Allied-Lyons plc.

The brewery had always been a large employer of labour in the town, with 200 men and 30 horses employed in 1863, rising to a workforce of 450 in 1908, which included 63 females in the bottling plant. Up till closure the site covered 20 acres with a work force of about 1,000. Many pages of facts and figures about the brewery could be included, but this is not really the purpose of this work. I am just picking out one or two interesting snippets.

*Pictorial World*, 9 August, 1888

A very severe storm in August, 1888, brought flooding to many parts of the borough, especially where there were rivers, which had a disastrous effect on the brewery. The river Rom flooded and the torrent of water swept through the brewery, causing substantial damage and washing away thousands of casks. The water was three feet high in the brewery yard. The barrels were swept all the way to the river Thames and it is said that between twenty and thirty thousand barrels were lost. These were mostly empty, but they included 400 barrels of newly brewed beer without bungs, with the whole consignment being ruined. The impressions of the flood appeared in *Pictorial World* the next week, which showed horses being rescued from the yard of the Angel public house, a stranded train at Chadwell Heath, barrels in the river Rom and the collapse of a barrel store at the brewery.

By good fortune the site of the brewery was well placed when the railway came to Romford in 1839. The brewery was able to expand its operation towards the railway line and to link into the Eastern Counties Railway system in 1853. For a start the railway wagons were hoisted from the brewery's own railway line up to the higher level of the Liverpool Street line. Later a line was built from the brewery under the embankment and up a gradient to a turntable, as the brewery line approached the main line at a right angle. By the turn of the century the turntable had been replaced by a curve, which meant that steam locomotives could take the beer directly into the Romford goods yard for onward transportation to any part of the country. Before the steam engines were introduced the wagons were pulled by horses within the brewery yards. Large scale redevelopment of the brewery started in the late 1950s, but the railway system survived until the mid 1960s. The old postcards of the brewery show the brewery's own railway system with the line leading towards Romford station to join the station's goods yards. The photograph was taken in the early part of this century.

The brewery railway system

# CHURCHES

There are 12 churches within the Borough which are Listed Buildings and these are -

Grade 1
St Andrew's Parish Church, Hornchurch
St Helen & St Giles Parish Church, Rainham
St Laurence Parish Church, Upminster
St Mary Magdalene Parish Church, North Ockendon

Grade 2*
St Edward the Confessor Parish Church, Romford
St Mary & St Peter Parish Church, Wennington

Grade 2
St John the Evangelist, Havering-atte-Bower
St Thomas Parish Church, Noak Hill
Church of St Andrew, Romford
All Saints' Church, Cranham
Salem Chapel, London Road, Romford
Upminster Old Chapel

There are, of course, many other churches in the area of various denominations some of which are also quite old, but for our purposes we will look at the Listed churches and start with a short history of how the church became established in the Havering area.

Although the Domesday Book does not actually record any churches within the fourteen manors that comprised what is now Havering Borough, it is generally believed that the majority of the parish communities had a church of some sort, although the priest would have worked for most of the week on his land or for the lord of the manor. Havering was half owned by the King, through his royal palace at Havering-atte-Bower, with his royal forest stretching all the way to the Thames, with the residue being thirteen manor estates on the eastern half of the borough, each with its own little population.

If there were Saxon churches in the villages at the time of Domesday in the 11th century, they were probably made of wood and it was not generally until Norman times that churches were built of stone or brick. The oldest standing church is St Helen & St Giles, Rainham, built in the 1170s and, although constructed 100 years after Domesday, it is a very good example of Norman architecture, as all the sections, chancel, nave, aisles and tower were all built at the same time, whereas in most churches there have been many additions over the centuries.

It was mentioned earlier that the royal palace was at Havering-atte-Bower and old records show that there were two royal chapels attached to the palace in 1250: both are shown on a plan of the palace dated 1578. The smaller chapel fell down with the rest of the palace about 1700. The larger chapel stood on the site of the present parish church and it probably originated as the King's chapel and part of the palace complex. From the Middle Ages, Hornchurch Parish Church, through the lord of the manor who owned the

Havering Chapel, rebuilt as St John's, Havering-atte-Bower, in 1878

St Andrew's, Hornchurch

Hornchurch, St. Andrew's Church (Showing Bull's Head.)

The Virgin Mary & St Edward
the Confessor, Romford, 1850

St Andrew's, Romford

15

church, appointed the chaplain at Havering chapel. It seems that of the two chapels at the royal palace, one was for the personal use of the royal household and called St Edward's, with the other for public worship and called St Mary's chapel.

St Mary's was finally demolished in 1876, although it is felt that the last building had only been substantially rebuilt about 1725/75. The new church was consecrated in 1878, having been rebuilt on the same site in the name of St John the Evangelist. The construction is brick faced with flint on a traditional style with an embattled south west tower. It is said that much of the brick came from the previous church. The cost was £5,276, with the main subscribers being David McIntosh, lord of the manor of Havering, and Mrs Pemberton-Barnes. The church font dates from the 12th century.

Hornchurch's church was referred to as the 'church at Havering', which existed in 1163, when Henry II gave it to a new priory which had been set up in Hornchurch. The priory was dissolved in 1391, when its land and possessions were purchased by William of Wykeham, Bishop of Winchester, who endowed the estate to New College, Oxford. The church was referred to as Havering's church, as it was originally all part of the royal manor estate of Havering-atte-Bower. The church was completely rebuilt in the 13th century, although almost a further rebuild took place in the 15th century, with some further additions in 1802. The nave arcades and the three clergy seats in the chancel are all that remain from the 13th century. The tower was built in 1491-2 with the spire being built at the same time. C T Perfect though, in his history of Hornchurch, thought that the spire was built a little later than the tower. The church is built of ragstone and septaria (limestone) with parts in brick.

Romford's first church was St Andrew's chapel, which was first mentioned in 1177 and which was situated just to the east of the river Rom on the south corner of Oldchurch Road and South Street. It is thought that mediæval Romford was sited to the west of the chapel in Oldchurch Road and this may also have been the site of the Roman settlement of Durolitum, although the exact location is not known. By the early 15th century, the centre of Romford had moved to the market place and consequently King Henry IV gave permission in 1406 for the inhabitants to build a more convenient chapel, which was dedicated to St Edward the Confessor. 'The King... considering the inconvenience under which the tenants of our manor at Havering, residing in the town of Romford, continually labour and for the convenience of the aged and feeble persons there, inasmuch as the chapel of Saint Andrew... is situated half a mile beyond the aforesaid town; by reason whereof our said chapel is frequently damaged and spoiled; we have granted... our said subjects... that, by the assent and authority of their diocesan, they may remove the said chapel from the place where it now stands to another part of the common near to the highway on the east side of the town... and take for their use certain oaks growing in the place where the said chapel shall be so newly erected.'

The chapel of St Edward was pulled down when the present church was built. The new church, on the same site, was also dedicated to St Edward and consecrated on September 19th, 1850, by the Bishop of Rochester. The original plan was to build the new church at

Salem Church, London Road, Romford

St Laurence, Upminster

Upminster Old Chapel,
St Mary's Lane

the other end of the market place. Work started in 1844, but was abandoned due to lack of funds and the site was converted into a cemetery. The new church is built with Kentish ragstone with Bath stone dressings in the Decorated style and was designed by John Johnson. The spire is 162 feet high compared with Hornchurch, at 120 feet. Two new vestries were added in 1885 and the church has remained virtually unchanged since.

Twelve years after the new St Edward's church was built in the market place, a new church of St Andrew was built in St Andrew's Road, Romford, in 1862. The designer was also John Johnson. The church was built to serve the new working class district that had grown up around the old barrack ground south-west of the town centre. The construction is of Kentish ragstone in the Early English style. Since the Second World War the area served by the church has once again been redeveloped.

Not far from St Andrew's is Salem Church in the London Road. This Baptist chapel also served the old barrack ground, which incidentally was the popular name for that part of Romford to the west of Waterloo Road, which was the Cavalry Barracks. In 1795, during the war with France, barracks for six troops of cavalry were built in the London Road, extending southwards along Waterloo Road. They were demolished in 1825. Salem church was built in 1847 to serve the new residential population following the closure of the barracks.

The church of St Thomas in Church Road, Noak Hill, was built in 1842 as a memorial to Frances, the wife of Sir Thomas Neave, Bt. of Dagnams, Harold Hill. It is a relatively small church built of red brick with a south-west tower. The designer was George Smith and it was built in the Early English style.

Churches are usually located near to manor houses and it seems strange in the case of Upminster that the parish church is mid-way between the old manor houses of Upminster Hall and Gaynes. There is a theory that the first church may have served a much larger area than just Upminster and possibly dates from before the Norman Conquest to serve the Hornchurch area as well. The first reference to the church was in 1223 and it was probably not long before this date that the first stone church was built, with any previous building being of wood. All that remains today of that first stone structure is evidence of 12th century stonework in the tower. With the exception of the tower the church of St Laurence was almost completely rebuilt in 1861-62. There were eastern extensions to the church in 1928 and 1937. The arcade which dates from c.1300, separating the nave and the north aisle, was one of the few pieces of the old church incorporated into the 19th century rebuild. The church font came from Upminster Hall, where the monks of Waltham Abbey had a chapel attached to their manor house.

Upminster has a second Listed church, now known as the Old Chapel, on the south side of the brow of Upminster Hill, almost opposite the windmill. The chapel was built in 1800 as a Congregational chapel for 300 persons, although preaching took place before that date in homes of local residents. The present front to the chapel is dated 1847 in the form of a Tuscan porch. In 1911 a larger stone church was built in Station Road, Upminster. The chapel was sold to the Plymouth Brethren when the Congregation church moved

St Mary Magdalene, North Ockendon

St Thomas's, Noak Hill

St Mary & St Peter, Wennington

19

premises. The building is now in private ownership and very dilapidated. It is undergoing repair, but may not be worth saving - which would be a pity.

The first known church at Cranham dates from the 13th century and the next complete rebuild was not until 1873-75 on the same site. Records show that during its life of about 600 years the church had, like most, various additions and alterations and it seems that when rebuilt it was said 'to be in a miserable state of dirt and dilapidation'. The present church was also dedicated to All Saints and was designed by Richard Armstrong. The cost was £5,114 of which the majority was given by Richard Benyon of Cranham Hall. A few monuments were retained from the old church, including a marble tablet to General Oglethorpe. Reference to this notable gentleman is found under Cranham Hall.

We said earlier that it was most likely that the majority of the Domesday manors of 1086 had some sort of church and this is borne out in the case of North Ockendon, where it is noted that there was a church attached to the manor house in 1075, when the manor was held by Westminster Abbey.

A point of interest, relative to most of the parish churches, is the appointment of the cleric, which in the main was held by the lord of the manor. The advowson, the right to appoint to a church living, passed from lord to lord, although occasionally this right passed to someone outside the parish, usually by way of sale. In North Ockendon's case the advowson rested with the lords of the manor from the 15th to the 20th centuries, before being passed by the Benyon family to the Bishop of Chelmsford. In the case of St Laurence, Upminster, the advowson was purchased by William Holden of Birmingham in 1780, with five successive family members all being rectors. From the Middle Ages the clergy were not paid a salary, but benefited from right to tithes that went with the living. The usual situation was that the rector could claim one tenth of the income of a parishioner either by way of cash or kind. A tithe barn was usually on glebe land (church land) near to the church and it is a popular misconception that the so-called Tithe Barn at Upminster Hall, which is now the agricultural and local history museum, was used for the collection of tithes. In Upminster's case the right to the collection of tithes was always held by the rector of St Laurence. Over the centuries there were always problems regarding what was a fair price to pay and fortunately this was all brought to a conclusion in 1836 by the Tithe Commutation Act, which did away with the payment of tithes, turning this charge into rates levied by the local authority. The clergy were then paid a salary.

Getting back to North Ockendon, the church of St Mary Magdalen still has its 12th century Norman doorway, which is all that is left of the first stone church. The majority of the present church dates from the 13th to 15th centuries with the tower also built in the 15th century. Like most churches restoration and improvements took place in the 19th century, with the lord of the manor, the Benyon family, meeting the cost. The Poyntz Chapel on the north side of the chancel was the burial place for successive lords of the manor, with the most notable being Sir Gabriel Poyntz, who had created memorials to his own ancestors, as well as to himself. There are eight small memorial tablets commemorating seven generations of the Poyntz family. This rural church deserves a visit, as do all the

Listed churches, as one cannot do justice in this volume in respect of all the other interesting items within the churches, like the various memorials to other noteworthy residents together with detailed information concerning church plate, the bells and historic church furniture. A whole volume could be written on just these twelve churches.

The Domesday Book states that a priest held half a hide (60 acres) at Rainham, which indicates that the church was established in at least the 11th century, with the present church, as mentioned above, having been built in the 1170s. St Helen & St Giles, which is a unique dedication in England, is constructed of septaria and flint rubble with ashlar dressings (stone facings). Although the main structure has remained unchanged through the centuries, many minor alterations have taken place. The bowl of the font is 12th century Norman, although some historians feel that it may be Saxon, adding weight to the theory that a church existed in Rainham 1000 years ago.

Like North Ockendon, Wennington's church in the 11th century was held by Westminster Abbey, with the present structure being of mediæval origin. The oldest part is the 12th century round arched doorway reset in the vestry. The are masoned blocks of limestone set into the floor of the nave, which were exposed in 1960 and are of, at least, Norman origin and could be of an earlier period. St Mary & St Peter stands in the Wennington Road and is built of rubble with limestone dressing.

St Helen's & St Giles, Rainham

All Saints, Cranham

21

St Edwards, Romford (and the Cock & Bell Inn)

## CHURCH HOUSE

The oldest building in Romford Market Place is undoubtedly Church House, which dates from 1480. The building was previously known as the Chantry House and then was a public house. Later it was a shop, before being bought by the church in 1908 and renamed Church House.

The building has jettying, which is the projection of the first floor joists up to two feet beyond the first floor walls. This had the effect of enlarging the area of the first floor rooms and afforded some protection from the weather for those sheltering under the projections. The jettying is still visible on the church side of the building, but in the 18th century the front of the building was extended towards the market to form a shop front by filling in the overhang.

The exact date of construction is not known, but it does seem that the property may have been built in 1480, when it was acquired by Avery Cornburgh as a house for a chantry priest, which he had founded in St Edward's church. Cornburgh was lord of the manors, Dagnams and Gooshayes, which cover all that area now Harold Hill. He founded a chantry in the chapel at Romford, which would involve the setting up of an altar in the building, in order that the chantry priest could say prayers for the souls of the departed. The endowment also provided for the provision of a property for the priest, which became known as the Chantry House. The benefaction also stipulated that the priest was to be a Doctor or Batchelor of Divinity or a Master of Arts who was to, in addition to his responsibilities at Romford, preach two sermons every year in the churches at South Ockendon, Hornchurch, Dagenham and Barking.

The 16th century saw the reformation of the church and the dissolution of the religious houses and, consequently, the suppression of the chantry at Romford. In 1547, the income derived from the chantry and the house itself became part of the Gidea Hall estate of Sir Anthony Cooke. Edward VI was now king and Cooke obtained the property due to the fact that he was tutor to the prince before he came to the throne. By 1613 the property was known as the Cock and Bell public house and by the 18th century it had become a shop. Since 1908 it has been owned by the church with its present use being for parochial purposes.

## CRANHAM HALL

Cranham Hall is approached by The Chase, an unmade road leading off St Mary's Lane. This narrow country lane leads to Cranham church, which is adjacent to the Hall, and, what with the nearby farm buildings, this whole area is a little piece of rural Essex on the edge of suburban Havering. As with many old manor houses, the church and the house are very close and, in Cranham Hall's case, there is a small gate leading directly from the Hall into the churchyard.

It is known that there was a house on the site in about 1600 and, although the history of Cranham manor dates back to the Domesday Book, it is believed that previous manor houses may have been located in the northern part of the parish. The present house was built about 1800 and incorporates a small portion of the previous building. The house faces east with five bays as shown in the photograph and is best viewed from the footpath to the pond east of the house.

A number of notable people have been connected with Cranham Hall through the centuries, starting with the Bishop of London in 1086, at the time of the Domesday Book. It is unlikely, though, that the Bishop ever resided at Cranham, as this was just one of many manors he held on behalf of William the Conqueror, as a reward for his support following the overthrow of King Harold. Sir William Petre of Ingatestone Hall and Thorndon Hall held the manor in 1571, when it comprised 780 acres, which was just under half of the whole acreage of the parish.

The most famous resident, though, was General James Oglethorpe. The Petre family had sold the estate to Sir Benjamin Wright and it was the daughter of one of his successors that married the General. He came to live at Cranham Hall in 1765 for the last twenty or so years of his life, dying in 1785. He is buried at the church, only a few yards from where he spent many happy years, after an illustrious career. Following University at Oxford he joined the army and, after a successful campaign against the Turks, entered Parliament as member for Haslemere, the seat previously held by his father. This sedentary life did not suit him and so he obtained a grant and a royal charter, together with a grant of land, to colonise a further part of America up the Savannah river in an area between South Carolina and Florida. The settlement, which he named Georgia in honour of King George II, was secured in 1732.

This large estate lasted until 1867, when 812 acres of farm land were separated from the Hall upon sale to Richard Benyon and it is on this land that the modern development of Cranham took place.

Cranham Hall
Listed walls of Cranham Hall

Crouches Farm

Cranham Court

## CRANHAM'S HOUSES

Cranham is a small, narrow parish that lies between Upminster and roughly the line of the M25 motorway, as it passes north/south through the Borough. Cranham's population hovered around the 400 mark during the 19th century, with everyone living in farms or cottages in the three principal roads of St Mary's Lane, Front Lane and Back (now Moor) Lane. Consequently, there were few large houses and only three were named on the Chapman and André map of 1777. Cranham Hall and Cranham Rectory are dealt with separately, which leaves Beredens, which was a manor house in the north of the parish. When the Arterial Road (A127) was built in the 1930s, this cut in two Front Lane and Moor Lane, with the northern section of these roads being renamed Beredens Lane and Folkes Lane respectively. The manor house of Beredens lay to the west of Beredens Lane to the north of where this road is now bisected by the M25. The estate, although in Cranham, was very close to the Great Warley parish boundary and there has always been a close association with principal landowners of that parish. The manor was formed out of Cranham Hall manor and dates back to at least the 14th century. At its peak, in 1801, the estate comprised 460 acres, of which 338 were in Cranham and the rest in Great Warley. In 1918 the estate was broken up with the manor house and some of the land being bought by the adjacent Goldings estate in Great Warley. In 1886 Beredens was described as 'an old restored manor house'. The house was destroyed in the 1939-45 War.

Cranham Hall and Beredens accounted for half of the acreage of the parish, with only four estates being over 100 acres in the early 19th century. The records do not name the other two, although one is likely to have been Crouches Farm, sited at the junction of Moor Lane and Front Lane, where the railway sidings are now. This farm and the surrounding land was owned by the railway company, who bought the farm when the line was being constructed from Upminster towards Southend. Even after the line was built they still retained the farm, probably looking ahead to a station at Cranham, which did not materialise, although the land eventually was used by London Underground as its sidings. The other large farm was possibly Mumfords, which became Westbury Farm, to the north of St Mary's Lane in the east of the parish.

The only other property of note, which still stands today, is Cranham Court, known as Cranham Holme when it was first built in the early part of this century. This large Edwardian house is now a nursing home for the elderly.

27

## COURT HOUSE

The Court House stood in Romford Market at the South Street end and the building was in the market place itself occupying a site in front of what is now a bank on the Market Place/South Street corner. Attached to the Court House were two shops extending to the South Street corner. There was a passageway behind the Court House, which ran in front of the other buildings in the market place. The last building on the site was a two storey Victorian edifice incorporating four cells on the ground floor, together with the court and ancillary offices. The building was pulled down in 1933 and, when one looks at the market place today with its wide open spaces, it is difficult to imagine that the Court House and two shops stood on what is now a pedestrian walkway and part of the market road.

Romford's Court House was different from others in the county, as the building was the location for the various courts that comprised the royal manor and liberty of Havering-atte-Bower. Reference is made under Havering Palace to this royal manor, stretching from the village of Havering-atte-Bower in the north to the Thames marshes in the south. The manor was in the Becontree Hundred, whereas other parishes in what is now Havering Borough were in Chafford Hundred. A Hundred, in historic times, was an administrative area, as we have Boroughs and Districts today. The manor of Havering, as it is usually called, belonged to the Crown from the 11th to the 19th centuries, although for administrative purposes it came to be a separate liberty by charter of Edward IV in 1465. Even before this date, Havering was occasionally referred to as a liberty and also sometimes treated separately from Becontree Hundred. In essence, the Liberty, like other royal manors, was an independent body with its own courts, rules and regulations. Successive monarchs confirmed the original charter although the documents refer to the area as the 'lordship or manor of Havering' and not the 'Liberty', which did not become the accepted style until the 18th century.

The charter established three courts to deal with cases occurring within the Manor or Liberty. These were the Quarter Sessions, which dealt with the more important cases, even up to murder, although in practise Romford's court tried very few serious cases, as crime was almost unknown in the area. There was also the Court Leet, meeting annually on Whit Tuesday, with cases concerning roads, commons, waste land and encroachments. Various officers were also appointed at this annual court, like the Clerk of the Market and the High Constables for Romford and Hornchurch. The most used and most important court, though, was the court of Ancient Demesne, held every third Thursday by the High Steward of the Manor, to deal with many sundry matters like debts, covenants, trespass, with the court also able to recognise the transfer of land. Once again, the records show that the court had little work to do at its three-weekly sittings and it was in 1828 that the Crown sold the lordship to a private person, which then gave the Crown no say in the appointment of Justices for the Courts. This made no difference to the Liberty Court, as little work was being done anyway. By the mid-19th century the passing of various pieces of legislation diminished the independence of the Liberty and these included the establishment of the county police force and the county courts, so that much of the work previously conducted was taken away from the Liberty courts. The Inclosure Act of 1811 had also left little scope for the Leet Court, but the Liberty and its courts survived until the end of the 19th century, when the Local Government Act of 1888 placed the administration of Havering under Essex County Council. Few privileges remained for the Liberty, which was finally abolished in 1892. The *Essex Times* recorded the last Quarter Sessions of the Liberty, when two prisoners were to come for trial. Presumably they were being held in Chelmsford Gaol, as they missed the train from Chelmsford and had to make the journey by road, arriving 90 minutes late. One of the men was convicted of stealing three rabbits and was sentenced to ten months hard labour. This seems a harsh sentence, but he did have previous convictions. The other man received ten years for stealing two live bullocks. This man also had led a life of crime, having already spent ten years in prison. Following the dissolution of the Liberty, Havering's Justices were transferred to the Essex bench and the Coroner for the Liberty also became an officer of the county.

The Court House was first mentioned in 1484 as being in Romford South, but historians feel that the site was in the market place. As early as the 13th century there was some kind of gaol in Romford. The Court House and gaol were rebuilt between 1737 and 1740 in the market place, but, by 1790, the cells were not being used, probably due to their poor state of repair. It is quite clear that by the end of the 18th century, the whole building was once again in need of renovation. Rebuilding did take place in 1826, with the first drawing showing what the earlier building looked like, and the second drawing showing the new building which lasted nearly a century. The quarter sessions were held in the market place until 1870, before being transferred to a new county court in South Street. The gaol and its four cells on the ground floor remained in use until a new police station was also built in South Street in 1894. When the Liberty was abolished in 1892, the Court House was sold by Mrs McIntosh, who held the manor of Havering, to the Romford Local Board, which was the name of the new local authority. The building was used as council offices until 1931.

Old Court House                              New Court House

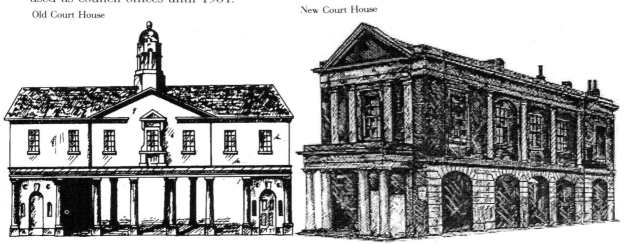

## DAGNAMS, incorporating COCKERELLS and GOOSHAYS

The three historic manors of Dagnams, Cockerells and Gooshays comprised what is now Harold Hill and accounted for all the land between the Colchester Road (A12) and Noak Hill Road to the north and east/west from Maylands golf course to Straight Road. Early records refer to the estate as Dagenhams, but in the 15th century it seems to have changed its name to Dagnam or Dagnams, probably to avoid any confusion with Dagenham parish in the Becontree Hundred.

At the time of the Domesday Book, the whole of the area was mainly forest and part of the King's royal manor of Havering-atte-Bower. By the 15th century, the only properties would have been the three mentioned above and, although in later centuries other properties were built, they were only farm houses and paid rent to one of the big three estates.

Dagnams first appeared when the name was mentioned in a survey of 1250 for Havering manor. Even at that time the estate comprised 500 acres. The name seems to have come from the tenant of the royal manor called Thomas of Dagenham, who held this acreage on behalf of the king. It looks as if this man came from Dagenham parish. Thomas was also the bailiff of Havering manor at the time of Edward I. The size of the estate grew slowly and in 1633 there were 703 acres. It was not until the Neave family purchased the estate in 1772 that we see substantial growth and by 1846 there were 1700 acres. By 1876 the acreage was over 1,800, peaking out at 2,200 acres in 1919, when the estate was owned by Sir Thomas L H Neave. Of this total, about 1,500 acres were sold, leaving the 550 acres of the house and grounds of Dagnams. The residue was sold in 1948 by his son to the London County Council, who also bought by compulsory purchase the other farmland that his father had sold previously.

During some 700 years, there have been many houses standing on the same site. The property was in the northern part of what in now Dagnam Park and the best way to find the exact location is to walk down Lower Noak Close, off Chequers Road, Noak Hill, and take the footpath due south, without turning left towards the M25. Small remains of the site are still visible and, by continuing walking southwards, you eventually come out into the park by the pond with the excellent views the owners would have had looking down towards the Colchester Road. The earlier properties were built within a moat and consequently there must have been spring water to achieve this effect in view of the high location of the property. The present pond is probably fed in this way and this could have been the source of the water supply. We know that there was a house built in Elizabethan times which had three high gables and was built of red brick. A new house was built and the moat filled in about 1660, when Sir Henry Wright bought the estate. The new house faced north, with the main drive running out to Noak Hill. Samuel Pepys visited Dagnams on several occasions around 1665 and described the house as 'a most noble and pretty house that ever, for the bigness, I saw'. Pepys records that he travelled to Dagnams from Deptford across the Thames at the Isle of Dogs by a ferry that was capable of taking a coach and six horses.

The Chelmsford/London coach passing the gates of Dagnams

Gooshays

He goes on to say that on the return journey the party lost its way and, having missed the ferry, had to sleep the night in the coach. They had brought food and wine with them for the journey and he says that during the night they became 'mighty merry'. When Sir Richard Neave purchased the estate in 1772 the house was rebuilt once again, which took four years to complete. The house was built of whitish grey brick and the style was late Georgian. This mansion faced south towards the Colchester Road, with a drive proceeding due south from the house, meeting the main road about where Dagnam Park Drive is today. There was a Lodge house at this point. Another drive went northwards, presumably along the same route as previous drives and joined Chequers Road at Noak Hill. The photograph of the painting of the coaching scene is interesting, as the coach is passing the gates and lodge of Dagnams in about the 1820s on the main Brentwood-London road (A12). The painter was James Pollard, whose speciality was mail coaches of the day. It is known that the coach featured is the Norwich-London coach, which was driven by the late coachman to Sir Thomas Neave of Dagnams, which is probably why the artist featured the lodge in his painting. Prior to the first World War, a later Sir Thomas Neave employed over 40 staff both in and outside the house. During the Second World War, the house was used by the Army. At one point, after the estate was purchased by the London County Council, it was planned to preserve the house, but this did not come about and it was finally demolished in the early 1950s.

Like Dagnams, COCKERELLS took its name from a 13th century tenant although the manor was added to the Dagnams manor in the late 14th century and consequently there is little specifically recorded about Cockerells after that date. The house was sited about half a mile due south of Dagnams and the drive from Dagnams would have passed very close to the property. The location of the house was just beyond Dycorts Junior School, off Dagnam Park Drive. Cockerells in 1633 was a large gabled building, which stood on the outside of a moated site and one wonders if earlier buildings stood inside the moat, as was usual in the Middle Ages, for protection purposes. The moated site is now an Ancient Monument and can be found on the edge of Dagnam Park, near Dycourts School. The property became known as Dagnam Park Farm in the 19th century and was finally demolished in 1948 to make way for housing development.

The earliest record of GOOSHAYS was in 1334, when the manor held 64 acres, although the records show that, by 1485, the manor held 1100 acres. The house and estate was sold to Sir Thomas Neave of Dagnams in 1829 and, like Cockerells, it became part of the Dagnams estate. With this purchase the Neave family owned all the land on which Harold Hill now stands, although the farm had reduced to only 287 acres. Gooshays farm house stood at the end of a long tree lined drive, which is now Gooshays Drive. The exact date of building of the last house is not known but its architecture was late Georgian, which places it about 1770-1790. The previous house on the site faced east, whereas the last house faced south down the drive. Nothing is known about the previous house, except that the walls were very thick and it does indicate that this manor house, which probably dated from mediæval times, was built as a fortress. London County Council acquired the property in 1947, along with the other parts of the Harold Hill area. Like Dagnams it was intended to preserve the farmhouse and for a time it was used as a community centre, but, due to vandalism and general decay, the house became unsafe and was pulled down in 1961.

We had said earlier that out of the three original manors of Dagnams, Cockerells and Gooshays there had evolved various farms in later centuries and when the last Neave sold the whole estate to the LCC in 1947/48 the following farms were included in the sales.

|  |  |
|---|---|
| Brick Kiln or Hilldene farm | - 112 acres |
| Harold Hill farm | - 137 |
| Manor farm | - 77 |
| Gooshays farm | - 266 |
| New Hall farm | - 139 |
| Harold Wood farm | - 50 |
| Dagnam Park farm | - 170 |

Dagnams

Dagnam Park farm was the old Cockerells manor house and New Hall farmhouse became The Morris Dancer public house, in Melksham Close, off Gooshays Drive. New Hall farm can trace its history back to at least 1461, when it was part of Gooshays manor and this was probably the first farm to be created out of the three principal manors. The house standing today was built between 1625 and 1675 and there was undoubtedly a house there previously. The house is of unusual design, as it is really two houses built side by side, but built as one property. This can be seen by the two separate roof structures. The house did have a priest's hole which was approached from a wooded spiral staircase and the room beyond contained a deep niche in the wall in which the priest would hide and not be seen by someone making a cursory search. The house was acquired by the LCC in 1947 and converted into a public house.

To complete this area of Harold Hill, mention must be made of The Priory, a large Victorian red brick house built about 1840 at the corner of Noak Hill Road and Lower Noak Close. The house was built by the Neaves of Dagnams as a Dower house for widows of the Neave baronets. The Priory had 41 acres and was eventually sold to the LCC in 1947 and the house was later demolished.

## DAMYNS HALL

Damyns Hall, one of Rainham's lesser known houses, was destroyed by fire in 1965. The farmhouse was situated in the north east of the parish, off the Aveley Road, just north of the junction with Warwick Lane/Bramble Lane. Even quite modern maps of the area still show the farm, which has now been long gone. The house was a long way from the centre of Rainham and is almost on the border of Upminster parish and consequently historians in the past have not documented much of the history of this old property. The last house on the site of Damyns Hall dated from the 17th century, with the name deriving from William Danyon who lived there in 1450. It is a pity therefore that not more is known about this old Rainham property, whose history goes back to at least the 15th century. The drawing of Damyns Hall is taken from a painting of the house done in the early part of this century. Originally the house was 'L' shaped, but part was taken down earlier this century, as evidenced by the large blank wall. The house had 16 rooms, including six bedrooms and three reception rooms. Owners this century were the Vellacott family, followed by Mr Ansell and then Olley Sand & Gravel. The farm was tenanted and farmed by three generations of the Paveley family from 1887 until the 1960s, when the land was then used for gravel winning.

## DURY FALLS

In the Middle Ages there were manor houses on twelve sites in Hornchurch, one of these being Lees Gardens, in Wingletye Lane, where Lee Gardens Avenue is today. The manor stretched from the Upminster Road in the south to the Southend Arterial Road (A127) in the north. There was built at the southern extremity a house which became to be called Dury Falls, on the corner of Wingletye Lane and Upminster Road. This corner was known from the 18th century as Doggett's Corner, probably after Mr Doggett, a churchwarden in 1779, who presumably also lived at Dury Falls.

This property has a history which goes back to the 13th century, as the name of the house appears to have been taken from the family of Doryval, who lived in this part of Hornchurch at that time. The present house is an early 17th century timber framed house, with a rather unusual construction, as the whole house has been built on a framework of solid balks of roughly hewn oak. The house was extended and altered in the 19th century, with further extensions in recent years on conversion to a residential home for the elderly. Until recently the house has been fairly small with no notable owners, apart from Mr Thomas Gardner, Chairman of the Parish Council for a number of years, a Justice of the Peace, a County Councillor and Chairman of the Hornchurch School Board, who resided there in the 1890s.

## FAIRKYTES

*The Victoria History of Essex* records Fairkytes as being in existence from about 1520 although the present house was built in the mid-18th century. The property is in Billet Lane opposite the Queen's Theatre. The front of the house is Victorian as the original house only had five bays with the mid nineteenth century front extending the property southwards by adding two further windows and a new wing.

Opposite Fairkytes was an iron foundry, which took its name from the house, which was sited where the Queen's Theatre is now. The founder of this business was Thomas Wedlake who lived at Fairkytes for some years after he came to Hornchurch in 1784. Joseph Fry lived in the property from 1870 to his death in 1896. He was the son of Mrs Elizabeth Fry, the Quaker, philanthropist and prison reformer. In the footsteps of his mother he contributed in his own way to the furtherance of good works in the area by being a notable benefactor of the village. During his time at Fairkytes he became the centre for all kinds of parochial and charitable work with Mr and Mrs Fry being ably assisted by their eleven children. One of their daughters, Augusta, followed in her grandmother's footsteps by becoming lady visitor at Holloway prison and also secretary to the Elizabeth Fry refuge fund in Hackney where she worked helping reform woman prisoners.

Fairkytes became the Hornchurch public library in 1953 and has also been used as council offices. It is now the Fairkytes Arts Centre.

## FOXHALL

Foxhall was built in 1718 and changed very little until it was pulled down for residential development in the 1930s. This Queen Anne/Georgian style country house had single storey wings added in about 1817 and it is unusual for a house to stand for over two hundred years with so few changes to its structure. The house stood in Corbets Tey Road, Upminster, at the foot of the hill which rises to Corbets Tey village. Although the house was demolished in the 1930s the land was not developed until after World War II and the surrounding garden wall remaining during this period. Foxhall Road now occupies the site. The house was more a country residence than a farm having at its peak only 60 acres spread over both sides of Corbets Tey Road. At the time of demolition the house and grounds were down to 14 acres. The most interesting owner of the property was Captain Philip Zachariah Cox who bought the lease for £2,090 in 1846. The freehold was held by Gaynes manor which he then bought for £150 giving him the freehold title. Captain Cox served in the 23rd Light Dragoons in the Napoleonic Wars and in particular at the battle of Talavera in Spain in 1809 and also at the battle at Waterloo in 1815. He died in 1858 at the age of 79 at Harwood Hall (which see). It appears that Captain Cox never actually lived at Foxhall preferring to reside at the larger house he owned at Harwood Hall. The house was called Osborne's in the early 18th century and subsequently Fox Hunter's Hall, before Foxhall or Fox Hall, as it was latterly known.

Fox Hall, Corbets Tey.

# FRANKS FARM

The best view of this very ancient site is from the M25 motorway, which is elevated as it passes over St Mary's Lane, Cranham in the far east of the borough. Historically Franks Farm fell within the parish of Great Warley, but in 1934 the parish was divided between the Urban Districts of Hornchurch and Brentwood when Franks Farm and a number of other old Warley houses were taken into what is now Havering. The property dates back to the Domesday Book of 1086 when it was known as Warley and later Warley Franks. The house today is fairly isolated, but in the 11th century the manor house supported a population of about 50 people. The owners can be traced right through the centuries and these are well recorded in the *Victoria History of Essex*. Great Warley was a long narrow parish of about five miles stretching from south of Brentwood to St Mary's Lane. The parish acreage was 2,890 of which Franks farm, as it was now known, comprised 640 acres at its peak in 1837. When the farm was part of the Benyon estate in the late 19th century it also included Codham Hall farm which although dating back to the 13th century was rebuilt by Benyon in yellow brick but this building does not have Listed status. The present Franks farm has been extended although many original beams have now been exposed. Previously the house had been cement screeded which was often the case a century or so ago. Parts of the house date from the 15th century, making it one of the oldest properties in the Borough.

## GERPINS and LAUNDERS

Launders is most likely to have been one of the four Rainham manors mentioned in the Domesday Book and the manor of Gerpins can be traced back to the end of the 12th century. The ancient manor house of Gerpins was moated and lay west of Gerpins Lane, Rainham at the bend of the road. The last house to stand on the original site was surrounded by a brick wall part of which stands today. This wall is Listed and dated about 1700. This particular manor house was demolished in the early part of the 19th century when a new house was built on the opposite side of the road. It was a large brick building with a square front, which was pulled down in the 1950s. Gerpins manor probably got its name from the French Jarpeville family that came from Gerpenville on the River Seine in the 13th century. The manor does not quite go back as far as the Domesday Book as it appears to have been originated in about the 12th century from land belonging to Rainham manor, the largest in the area, and pieces of other local manors. Records are available of most of the owners of the estate through the centuries with the majority being London businessmen. Latterly Gerpins was owned by farmers until the land was bought for gravel reclamation and use as the local rubbish disposal site.

Unfortunately even less is known about Launders which dates back to the Domesday Book. The probably location of the house was off Launders Lane, Rainham, to the east of this rural lane near to the site of Launders Barn, which fell down in the 1950s. Launders became part of the adjacent Berwick estate in 1789 and descended with that estate thereafter.

Gerpins Farm
(*photograph by Laurie Ford*)

# GAYNES MANOR

Although the manor was in existence in at least the 11th century it did not obtain its name until Vitalis Engayne acquired the manor in 1218. The most famous, or infamous, person to have held Gaynes was Alice Perrers. In the 14th century Edward III became captivated by Alice, who was in the service of the Queen, Queen Philippa. The King lavished gifts of money and land on Alice and she soon became a very powerful woman even to the extent of influencing the law of the land to her own ends. Parliament soon got fed up with her antics and passed a law forbidding women to practise in the courts. She was banished for a short period, but, following the King's death, she returned having married Sir William Windsore. Sir William supported Richard II in his war with France and for his services he was granted all the lands Alice had held when she was friendly with the previous King which included the manor at Upminster.

There seems to have been a problem with the title to Gaynes. Alice Perrers died in 1400, leaving Gaynes to her younger daughter Joan and other manors to her other daughter Jane provided that they could be recovered from her late husband's heirs as she considered that the estates had been acquired by the heirs illegally. It is recorded that Sir John Deyncourt held Gaynes in the late 14th century and, following his death in 1393, the estate passed to the King as his son, Roger, was a minor and could not hold land until he became of age. It seems that Edward III had given Gaynes to both Alice Perrers and Sir John Deyncourt. Joan Perrers' case was taken to court and the outcome was that Joan received an annual settlement for life provided the manor of Gaynes was surrendered to Roger Deyncourt.

In the 1540s Ralph Latham bought the estate then comprising 1,000 acres having fallen from about 1,600 acres (including forest) at the time of the Domesday survey. Ralph Latham also bought the Upminster Hall estate in 1543 which meant that he owned practically the whole of Upminster.

George Montgomery became the owner in 1749 when he drew up a map which showed that the estate still comprised most of the land in the southern part of Upminster. The manor house itself was off Little Gaynes Lane roughly at the end of Gaynes Court extending towards Tawney Avenue. The estate extended southwards from the centre of Upminster all the way to, and including, Stubbers in North Ockendon. The estate also took in Hactons at the end of Little Gaynes Lane and the New Place estate in St Mary's Lane.

Following Montgomery's death the manor was acquired in about 1780 by the Esdaile family, who were already leaseholders of part of the estate, which historians feel was Hoppy Hall, sited opposite Springfield Gardens in Corbets Tey Road. Sir James Esdaile was a wealthy London merchant and he started a building programme on his estate part of which still remains today. He built himself a new Gaynes mansion, the architect being James Paine, who was also the architect for Thorndon Hall (still standing) designed for Lord Petre in 1764. The mansion designed for Esdaile was described as being a mansion with two wings and having a lofty portico of the Corinthian order. The house was approached by winding steps on either side leading to the first floor level where the main rooms were

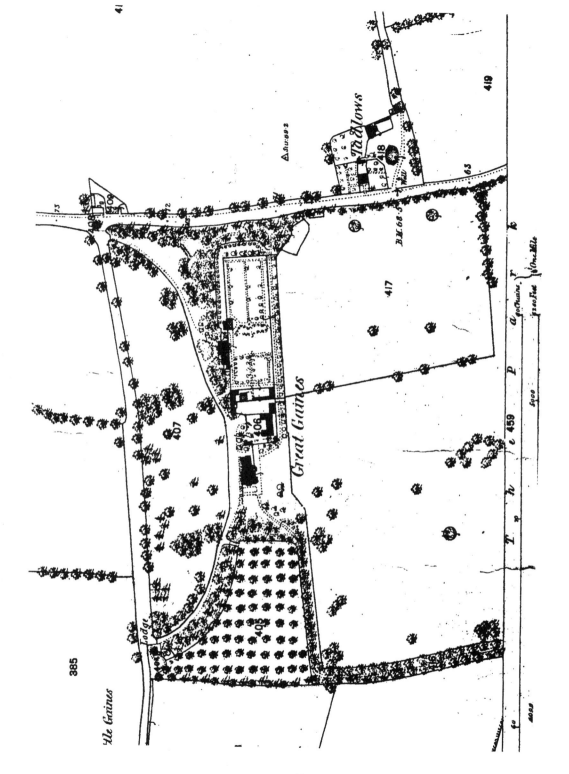

# UPMINSTER, ESSEX.

Within fifteen miles of the City, near the Station and adjacent to extensive development.

---

*Particulars, Plans and Conditions of Sale of the*

## VALUABLE FREEHOLD
## RESIDENTIAL AND BUILDING ESTATE

# Gaynes Park

EXTENDING TO

# Over 400 Acres

including the Mansion, standing in a Well-timbered Park, with Four Secondary Residences :

| | |
|---|---|
| **LITTLE GAYNES** | **LONDONS and** |
| **HOPPEY HALL** | **HUNTS** |

and FOURTEEN COTTAGES with nearly **Three Miles of Frontage** to main and parish roads.

**DRAINAGE, WATER, GAS, ELECTRIC LIGHT**
all available in the vicinity.          The Estate is

## *Ripe for Development*

on modern lines and, with the exception of the smaller houses and some of the cottages,

WILL BE SOLD WITH VACANT

## POSSESSION ON COMPLETION.

---

To be offered for Sale by Auction, IN ONE LOT, by

# ALFRED SAVILL & SONS

At the London Auction Mart, 155, Queen Victoria Street, E.C.,

On MONDAY, the 30th day of APRIL, 1928,

At 2.30 o'clock precisely.

---

SOLICITORS : Messrs. WESTERN & SONS, 35, Essex Street, Strand, W.C. 2.

AUCTIONEERS' HEAD OFFICE :          **51a, LINCOLN'S INN FIELDS, W.C. 2.**
Telephone : HOLBORN 4912 (4 lines).

THE ESTATES GAZETTE, LTD., KIRBY STREET, LONDON, E.C.

Londons

Hunts Farm

Hoppey Hall

43

Gaynes Park

Bridge at Parklands

located. This description is similar to that of Thorndon Hall and it is probable that the two properties looked very similar. It is unfortunate that this large house only lasted for about 40 years, for in 1820 it was demolished. Sir James Esdaile's other building projects included New Place in St Mary's Lane, Harwood Hall in Harwood Hall Lane, Corbets Tey. He also built Londons and Gaynes Lodge in Corbets Tey Road and various other smaller houses. The effect of this building programme was the development of the southern end of Upminster which in turn increased the population due to the number of servants and tradespeople required to look after the new houses. The population rose from 550/600 at the time Esdaile arrived in Upminster to 765 at the 1801 census.

After the demolition of all but the east wing of Esdaile's Gaynes the Reverend John Clayton built Gaynes Villa (later known as Little Gaynes) on a plot a little to the east of the old mansion in 1821. The east wing was finally pulled down and the Reverend George Clayton (son of John) built a new Gaynes in 1846 on the same site which meant that there was now a new Gaynes manor house and also Gaynes Villa, almost adjacent. The new Gaynes was nothing like its predecessor, as the photograph shows. In 1879 Henry Joslin bought Gaynes and tried to follow in Esdaile's footsteps and build up the estate which had been broken up when the old mansion was pulled down. He bought back Hoppy Hall farm with 98 acres and Hunts farm of 130 acres. Henry Joslin died in 1927 and this event signalled the demise of the last of Upminster's estates, as building development had already commenced in the northern part of Upminster following the break up of the Upminster Hall estate. The sale particulars of 1928 give an idea of the extent of Joslin's Gaynes estate with Harwood Hall, Gaynes Lodge and the stable block for New Place (the Clock House) still standing today as a reminder of the Esdaile building programme of the 1780s. Part of the park of Gaynes has been retained as Parkland Open Space, as a reminder of this large manor which dates back to the Domesday Book.

Gaynes Villa

45

# GIDEA HALL

One really cannot do justice to the history of Gidea Hall in a few pages, but if someone is interested in delving further into this fascinating part of Romford's history then one of the principal works of reference is I G Sparkes' *Gidea Hall and Gidea Park*. More information can be found in the *Victoria History of Essex (Volume VII)* and from the Essex Record Office in Chelmsford. For this short piece I will concentrate on the house itself, flavoured with some information about the principal people connected with it.

The map shows the location of the mansion, which was just behind where Gidea Park tennis club is today. The estate was quite extensive stretching from Gallows Corner in the east to Raphael's Park in the west. Northwards the estate extended to about where the Eastern Avenue passes through Rise Park. The whole comprised about 620 acres. Other features of the estate that still remain are the Spoon Pond immediately north of the house, now the tennis courts in the park, which are actually built in the indentation of the pond itself. At the northern end of the tennis courts is the childrens' playground, which is also built on low lying land, with the whole looking like a spoon. Reed Pond Walk takes its name from the pond which lay within this circular road which is now dried up and a copse. Moving to Heath Drive the photograph shows a piece of wall and gate entrance which was one of the entrances to Gidea Hall. Adjacent is the bridge over the road which looks on to the Fish Pond and Lotus Pond, which still remain, and which were features of the grounds of the house. Raphael's Park itself is fortunately a permanent reminder of the old estate together with the lake and the bridge in Main Road (Black's Bridge) which was specially designed with three arches to give the lake a pleasing character. Black's Bridge and the wall in Heath Drive are now Listed Buildings.

The history of Gidea Hall dates back to at least 1250 when the daughter of Simon of Gidiehulle (Gidea Hall) held land of the manor of Havering (Havering Palace). Sir Thomas Cooke purchased the manor in the 1460s and under a charter granted by Edward IV built a large new property which was referred to as a `castle' when the charter was drawn up. It took three generations of the Cooke family to complete the building over a period of 100 years and it ended up looking like the drawing of 1638. The first Cooke became Lord Mayor of London in 1462 and following reaching this pinnacle of success retired to Romford to start the rebuilding of Gidea Hall.

Sir Thomas Cooke was accused of supporting the previous Lancastrian regime (Henry VI) and ended up in prison. He died in 1469 but fortunately he was not deprived of his estate and his successors completed the rebuilding programme.

Cooke's Gidea Hall was a prestigious moated Tudor style mansion, although started before the Tudor period, built round a quadrangle. The four corners had small towers capped with domes with two larger towers within the building. The engraving shows a double arched bridge crossing the moat to the main entrance from a courtyard. The stables and other outbuildings were in a further courtyard to the side of the main house which is in the foreground of the engraving. The house remained unchanged for over 250 years, until the estate was purchased by Sir John Eyles who demolished the house and built a

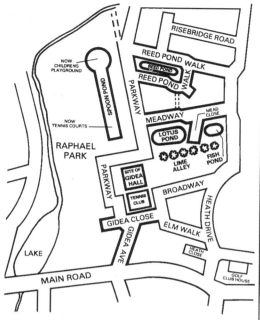

Marie de Medici's visit in 1637

LA SORTIE DE LA REYNE ACOMPAIGNE DV ROY DE LA
GRANDE BRETAIGNE SON BEAU FILS DV CHATEAV DE
GIDDE HALLE.

Gidea Hall, Romford.

47

Gidea Hall, as it was about 1730 (from an engraving by Humphry Repton)

mansion in Georgian style in 1720.

Gidea Hall was favoured on more than one occasion by royal patronage with Queen Elizabeth I visiting the house in 1568. In that year she made one of her 'Progresses' through London and Essex staying at Havering Palace where she spent two nights in July visiting Pyrgo Park while she was in Havering-atte-Bower. She then moved on to Gidea Hall for two further days where she was the guest of Sir Anthony Cooke.

The drawing we have of the house of 1637 is the only one in existence which was done by a Frenchman who was accompanying Marie de Medici on her way from France via Harwich to London, with an overnight stop at Gidea Hall. Apart from the King's country palace at Havering-atte-Bower, Gidea Hall was the largest mansion in the area capable of entertaining this important lady and her retinue. Marie de Medici was the Queen Mother (mother of Queen Henrietta/Charles I). Maria was also the widow of Henry IV of France and the mother of Louis XIII. Consequently she had a daughter on the throne of England and her son was King of France. Charles I travelled to meet his mother-in-law and stayed overnight at Havering Palace before proceeding to Chelmsford where he met Maria and then they both travelled together to Gidea Hall. The King though did not sleep the night at Gidea Hall, but returned to Havering Palace.

The new Gidea Hall and the last house on the site was also an impressive building although lacking the style of its Tudor predecessor. The rooms were exceptionally large having a drawing room of 35 feet by 21 feet and a library of 32 feet by 21 feet. The billiard room was on the first floor where there were six bedrooms two of which had two dressing rooms each, two had one dressing room each and two further bedrooms. The top floor had a nursery of four rooms, together with a further ten bedrooms, which presumably were the servants' quarters. There was stabling for 25 horses together with further space for six carriages under cover over which there was further servants' accommodation. The gardens contained the usual areas for vegetables and an orchard, together with a vineyard, melon ground and orangery. The lake and other features remaining today were all constructed at the time the new house was built. It was also at this time that the estate was increased in size from its then 200 acres to 600 acres.

The property changed hands many times during its life and by the mid-19th century it was occupied by two families. In 1896 Herbert Raphael bought the estate, but he did not live there himself. He was a wealthy man and devoted his life for the good of the community. In 1902 he gave the local authority part of the estate comprising 15 acres which became the Raphael's Park we know today. A further 450 acres were transferred for the building of the Gidea Park residential estate with further land being used to lay out the Romford golf course and the sports ground at Gallows Corner. During the 1914-18 War the house became the billet for the Artists' Rifles and in the late 1920s the house was used as tenement flats when housing was in short supply. This second large mansion on the site lasted 210 years before being pulled down in 1930, by which time it was almost surrounded by housing.

## GREAT HOUSE

One of the best known maps of Essex is that by Chapman and André of 1777, which is sufficiently detailed to show all the principal houses in each parish in the county. About ten houses are detailed by name in Upminster, including Great House, where a house still stands in the northern part of Hall Lane about a quarter of a mile from the junction with Nag's Head Lane. The house was pulled down in 1802 and the present one erected on the same site. To have featured in the 1777 map its predecessor was probably much larger and all that remained of the old property in the 19th century was evidence of a boating lake that had been formed out of damming a small rivulet that passed through the fields on its way to the river Ingrebourne.

Little is known about the history of this house and its occupants, apart from Sir William Clarke Hall, a barrister and magistrate, and his wife who came to reside and farm their 86 acres in Upminster in 1898. Sir William died in 1932, but his wife continued to live in the house, until she died in 1979 at the age of 100. In 1894 Lady Clarke Hall had entered the Slade School of Art, where she was an outstanding pupil. She continued her artistic career until 1947 and examples of her work can be seen at the Tate Gallery, Victoria & Albert and British museums and many more. In 1971 a retrospective exhibition of her work was held in London covering her 50 year career. She also published two books of poetry.

The house can be found in Tomkyns Lane, a narrow rural road running from the Southend Arterial Road (A127) coming out at Tylers Common. Originally the road was called Bird Lane, but following the construction of the trunk road dividing Bird Lane, the northern section of the road had its name changed.

Most history books refer to the property as a farm called Tomkyns, which was part of the Upminster Hall estate until 1908 when it was bought out of the estate for £300. In the late 19th century the farm comprised 74 acres. Great Tomkyns is one of the oldest properties in the borough and, like most old buildings it has undergone change through the centuries, although it still retains its timber framed hall rising the whole height of the house. The exact date of construction is not known but it is described as a 15th century yeoman's house in Pevsner's *Buildings of England*. The farm was previously called Great Readings and, in T L Wilson's *History & Topography of Upminster,* he says that during the American War of Independence (1775-83) a large quantity of timber was cut down on the estate for use by the navy for ship building. Adjacent to the house there is still standing a 17th century weatherboard barn.

Grey Towers
Grey Towers lodges

## GREY TOWERS

Grey Towers stood at the northern end of Grey Towers Avenue, at the Abbs Cross Road junction with Hornchurch Road. This crenelated mansion was the last large house built in Hornchurch and erected in a park of 50 acres by Henry Holmes in 1876. The present Abbs Cross Avenue was the house's driveway, which was lined with lime trees. Where the drive met the main road there were two lodge houses built in the same style as Grey Towers. The photographs show the house in about 1915 and the two lodges in the 1930s, after the house had been demolished and Grey Towers Avenue built. The lodges survived to about the 1960s with the plots still visible today.

Most of the photographs of the house show it overgrown with ivy and other creepers. The most impressive feature of the house was the black and white marble staircase which rose out of an impressive decorated hall. The hall's ceiling was carved oak and there was a fine stained glass window at the top of the first flight of stairs. The gardens were terraced due to the slope of the land leading down to Ravensbourne Brook which was made into an ornamental lake. The parkland was used for various local celebrations and within the grounds there was a cricket pitch which was used by the village cricket club.

Lieut. Colonel Henry Holmes D.L., J.P., came from a Durham Quaker family and was a shipbuilder in the north country. He had extensive business interests with his offices in London. He was a ship owner as well and also a director of a London bank and for some years joint proprietor of the Hornchurch Brewery (see Breweries). Prior to building Grey Towers Henry Holmes lived at Harwood Hall, Corbets Tey. Holmes was one of the most important men in the parish for about 30 years, during which time he held many local offices. He found time, notwithstanding his many business interests, to support the village of Hornchurch both as a community leader and also by way of his charitable bequests. Henry Holmes died at the age of 85 in 1913, Mrs Holmes died the next year.

With the outbreak of the 1914-18 war the house was taken over by the army and used as the headquarters and barracks for the First Sportsmen's Battalion (23rd Royal Fusiliers). The battalion was famous for the many and notable sportsmen who joined its ranks including county cricketers, top footballers, golfers, oarsmen and many more. The house and grounds later became the home of the New Zealand forces when it was used as a hospital and convalescent home. The house was finally demolished in 1931 to make way for residential development.

## HACTONS

Hactons is at the end of Little Gaynes Lane, Upminster where it meets Hacton Lane opposite the Optimist public house. The house, which lays back from the road, is basically as it was when built in about 1770 by William Braund. At the time of building it was one of the principal properties in Upminster and even when Sir James Esdaile rebuilt Gaynes mansion and started his building programme in Upminster Hactons still ranked as one of the largest half dozen properties.

Wilson in his *History & Topography of Upminster* gives a full description of the house, which was a red bricked building (now cement rendered) with stone quoins and dressings. The house has a central block and two wings which do not project forward as in most country houses but are flush to the main building The two wings are one storey high and unchanged but the main mansion originally had a portico which was approached by a flight of stone steps above which was an imposing ballustrated parapet and cornice. These embellishments have now disappeared and the present building looks rather ugly with a further floor having been built in post World War II times, where the parapet and cornice used to be. The building is now flats, but the drawing gives an idea how it once looked. Wilson says that the saloon occupied the whole depth of the house with only the central block being used by the family in residence with the two wings being the kitchens and servants' quarters.

William Braund was a wealthy London merchant and not one to be bullied by the lord of the manor at Gaynes. Braund had a dispute with Sir James Esdaile regarding the fencing in of a piece of ground in front of the house abutting the road which Braund said was to stop people falling into the ditch at night. Braund was forced to take the fence down but later Sir James himself fenced off a piece of land opposite where Upminster Junior School is now in St Mary's Lane where villagers had the right to water horses or livestock. Braund entered the newly enclosed land, watered his own horse and then took the gate off its hinges leaving it on the ground. Eventually, Sir James backed down with the villagers getting their watering hole back and William Braund his fence at Hactons.

In 1803, when Sir Thomas Lennard was in occupation, there was a review of the Barstable and Chafford Volunteer Cavalry Troop at Hactons of which Sir Thomas was Captain. A further interesting anecdote in connection with this house is that during World War II, at a time when the property was not occupied by the Army, it was found that trespassers were gaining entry through a secret passage leading from the grounds to a small room off the hall which had in it a movable dresser.

Hactons, as built
Hactons, now

# HARE HALL

Hare Hall is in Upper Brentwood Road, Gidea Park, and now forms part of the Royal Liberty School. The modern photograph shows that the façade has changed very little from the engraving of the 1800s. The first evidence of a property on this site dates back to about 1590 when a house and lands called Goodwins appears on the records of the Gidea Hall estate.

The present house was built in 1769 for John A Wallenger, to a design by James Paine, who also designed Thorndon Hall. The house style is typical of the period although it must have been one of Paine's smaller projects. The house is described as being in the Palladian style with its main north front having five bays attached to which were pavilions joined by short corridors containing the service rooms. The ground floor, referred to as the basement, was rusticated stone above which were two upper floors which accommodated the main rooms of the house. The front of the house is adorned with a giant portico and pilasters at the corners. The front is of Portland stone although the south front was constructed of brick with enlargements being made in 1896. The main rooms were on the first floor which were approached by a central staircase with curved ends and having an iron balustrade.

The Eastern Counties Railway Company had constructed the line from London to Romford, which opened in 1839, although three years earlier the company was buying land for the line's onward journey through Gidea Park and Harold Wood (see Railway Stations). The company was forced to purchase the whole of the Hare Hall estate of about 80 acres, although, of course, only a strip through the middle was needed. Attempts to sell off the residue of the estate were not too successful and consequently the railway company let Hare Hall to the engineer responsible for the section, Mr Braithwaite, whilst the work was in progress. The house and remaining land was eventually sold off in 1852 at a considerable loss to the company.

By 1897 the property was in a dilapidated condition but fortunately Mr Castellan bought the house and 71 acres and proceeded to renovate the estate and enlarge the house. During the 1914-18 war the house was requisitioned for military purposes with the estate being sold after the war when the land was used for residential development and the house became part of the Royal Liberty school in 1921. We are fortunate that the original north front remains virtually unchanged, although the interior is now mainly classrooms with little evidence of the large rooms of this old house. Many of the roads in the vicinity bear the names of past owners of Hare Hall - Wallenger, Severn, Pemberton, Western and Castellan.

Hare Hall

Royal Liberty School

## HARROW LODGE ESTATE

The Harrow Lodge estate comprised most of the area which is now Harrow Lodge Park, Hornchurch Road, together with the adjacent land upon which stood the St Leonard Children's Home and which is now a new residential development. Harrow Lodge is still standing and is approached through an avenue of trees leading from the main road. Historically the estate would have been part of the Suttons manor estate and possibly this area of nearly 100 acres was separated when Harrow Lodge was built in 1787. Although the park that we know today runs right the way through to Upper Rainham Road and totals 120 acres the Elm Park end was not part of the original estate but part of Maylards Green manor.

The house is a stuccoed two storey building with a slate roof. The original house was fairly small by standards of the day, although the estate which supported this farmhouse was also of no great size. The extension to the left of the house as shown in the photograph is more recent. In 1886 the estate of 86 acres was purchased by the Board of Guardians of St Leonard, Shoreditch, for £6,300. The Board provided homes and schooling for their destitute children. A self-contained village was built and opened in 1889 which contained, in addition to the houses and a school, an infirmary, swimming bath, bakery and workshops. Previously poor or orphaned children were housed in barrack room type accommodation and this new concept of individual houses with a 'family" and house-mother was quite revolutionary and forward thinking in those Victorian times. It seems that at that time Harrow Lodge and its large garden was let, with the 60 acres of unused fields (part of the park) being let to a local farmer.

The Children's Home was taken over by the London County Council in 1930 and in 1965 by the London Borough of Tower Hamlets. The Home acreage was sold for residential development, although the Village Hall had been given Grade 2 Listed status. At the time of writing it is still standing although in a state of disrepair and looking rather isolated among the new houses.

With the growth of Hornchurch in the 1920/30s it is fortunate that the local authority were able to purchase Harrow Lodge and the farmland and to develop the park right the way through to Elm Park to include the farmland that was part of the Maylards estate. Harrow Lodge was the main public library for Hornchurch from 1936 to 1953, when Fairkytes, Billet Lane, took over this rôle. The property is still owned by the local authority having had various uses in recent times.

Harrow Lodge

One of the 'family homes' at St Leonard's Children's Homes

## HARWOOD HALL

It is certain that there was a previous house on the site as evidenced by some very old beams within Harwood Hall, but our knowledge of the estate does not go back any further than about 1700, as most of the history of the house would be tied in with Gaynes manor of which it was part until 1819. Harwood Hall can be found in Harwood Hall Lane, Corbets Tey, with the present house having been built by Sir James Esdaile of Gaynes (see Gaynes manor) in 1790. It was built for his son-in-law, George Stubbs, and is described by the historian Wilson in the 19th century as a handsome embattled structure with a central bow. The hall, dining and drawing rooms are all spacious and well proportioned. Wilson says that the stone portico over the front door and also over the billiard room at the east end, which form wings, were brought from Great Myless, near Ongar, when that mansion was pulled down about 1860/70. Some interesting people have lived at Harwood Hall through the years. Sir Thomas Barrett Leonard resided there from 1801 to 1804 before he moved to Belhus in Aveley. In 1819 the house and grounds were bought out of the Gaynes estate by Captain P Z Cox (see Foxhall) who attempted to improve the grounds by importing fir cones from Rome, but unfortunately the saplings died when transplanted into the grounds. The house was rented by Henry Holmes before he moved to his newly built Grey Towers in Hornchurch (see Grey Towers).

## HAVERING PALACE

Havering Palace can trace its history back to the Domesday Book of 1086 and was in use by the monarchs of England until about 1638 when Charles I stayed there on his way to meet his mother-in-law who was travelling from the Continent to London via Harwich. Much research has taken place as to the exact location of the palace and it is now fairly certain that it was sited immediately behind the present parish church of Havering-atte-Bower which stands on the west side of the village green. It seems that with the coming of the Civil War in the 1640s and the abolition of the royalty in 1649 Havering Palace fell into disrepair. A survey of all the royal properties in 1650 described Havering as 'a confused heap of ruinous decayed buildings' whose materials of lead, glass, brick, tile and timber were only valued at £480. It is known that the Bower House in Havering-atte-Bower was built from materials from the palace in 1729 and by 1764 only part of one of the palace walls remained. It seems that by 1816 nothing remained at all. Although by 1650 the palace was no more, the land was retained by the Crown and the records show that the estate still contained just under 1,000 acres.

No drawing of the palace exists and the only plan of the building was that done by Lord Burleigh in 1578, which shows it to be group of about twelve two storey buildings all inter linked having pitched tile roofs. The first building on the site was constructed by Edward the Confessor in the 11th century as one of his country manors. Some historians feel that this royal house was very much like a Wild West fort with a palisade of tree trunks and possibly a moat surrounding the royal buildings, which would have been made of wattle and daub with thatched roofs. Ogborne's *History of Essex* says that Edward the Confessor's palace was built of 'free-stone' and leaded. Free-stone would have been sand stone or limestone that can be cut or sawn easily. With the Norman Conquest this brought into being the use of brick and stone more generally into building methods and in 1250 we note that building work on the palace included the building of a chimney in the Queen's chamber and also placing glass in the windows. Religious scenes were to be painted in the Queen's chapel, presumably on the walls, indicating that by this time the chapel was built of brick or stone. The King's stable was to be lengthened with the roof to be of shingles (probably wooden tiles).

A survey of the palace in 1596 at the time of Elizabeth gave some indication of the principal rooms which would not have been much different from Lord Burleigh's plan of 1578. There is mention of The Great Chamber, which would have been the principal reception room, The Presence Chamber, the Lord Chamberlain's lodgings, the Withdrawing Chamber, the Bed Chamber and two chapels (King's chapel and Queen's chapel). Mention is made of rooms for the Queen's lady in waiting and other ladies of the privy chamber together with all the usual kitchens and pantries that went with any large country house. The survey also gives a little detail of the contents of the rooms with mention of floor matting, tables, cupboards and whether the room had a lock and key which most did. In the bakehouse the survey records that there was a kneading trough and four moulding boards. The survey also confirms the location of the palace when it mentions the palace

Gatehouse next to the Green, which must have been an imposing entrance as it had a lodgehouse over the gatehouse. It is noted that all the windows for all the rooms were glazed and it is clear that in the 16th century the palace was at its peak in terms of size and the standard of its appointment. The Royal Accounts show that the two chapels boasted stained glass windows as early as the mid-13th century when Henry III ordered that windows of both chapels be made showing Shields of Arms of his family. This order to the Master of the King's Works was also requested for Westminster Abbey where the shields can still be seen to this day in the north and south choir aisles.

Although this book is principally about historic buildings it would be an oversight if no mention was made of the royal visits to Havering Palace. There are many works of reference which detail all the royal visits and so I will just summarise the use that the Kings and Queens of England made of this rural Palace, which can be equated with Sandringham today.

| | | |
|---|---|---|
| Edward the Confessor | 1042-66 | Built Havering Palace |
| Henry I | 1100-36 | Much used by Queen Matilda |
| John | 1199-16 | 12 visits in 17 year reign |
| Henry III | 1216-72 | 21 visits |
| Edward II | 1307-27 | Isabella, grand-niece married in royal chapel 1321 |
| Edward III | 1327-77 | 30 visits between 1331 & 1337 |
| Richard II | 1377-99 | Only occasional visitor |
| Henry IV there | 1399-13 | Much used by Queen Joanne, who as a widow lived and died |
| Henry VI | 1422-61 | At least 4 visits |
| Henry VIII | 1509-47 | Katherine of Aragon held the manor until her divorce; Anne Boleyn visited in 1531; Elizabeth and Mary, children of Henry VIII, lived at Havering |
| Edward VI | 1547-53 | Died aged 16 but was nursed and spent much time at Havering |
| Mary I | 1553-58 | Only one visit as Queen |
| Elizabeth I | 1558-03 | Many visits including 6 before the Spanish Armada battle |
| James I | 1603-25 | Frequent visitor |
| Charles I | 1625-49 | Last monarch to sleep at Palace in 1638 |

This shows that the palace at Havering was a favourite retreat for the royal family for about six hundred years until it fell into decay by 1650. During the Commonwealth some of the land and possessions of Charles I and Queen Henrietta were sold, which included Havering Palace, which was divided into two lots (east and west). The east division totalling 497 acres, including the site of the manor house sold for £4,733 with the larger west division, which contained much forested land, selling for £4,158. With the restoration of the monarchy in 1660 the land was reclaimed by the Crown, but leases were now granted to various people effectively finishing the royal link with Havering-atte-Bower.

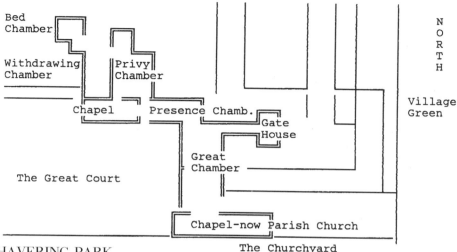

Bed Chamber

Withdrawing Chamber

Privy Chamber

Chapel

Presence Chamb.

Gate House

Great Chamber

The Great Court

NORTH

Village Green

Chapel-now Parish Church

The Churchyard

## HAVERING PARK

It can be seen from the story of Havering Palace that, following the royal link being broken, after the old palace has fallen down, that the land had eventually been leased by the Crown and divided into farms. It seems that the farms assumed names like Manor Farm or Bower Farm and there are various references to `Havering Park' in the years before the mansion that we now know as Havering Park was built. It does not appear though that there was another property called Havering Park as these references probably just refer to farm land that was once part of the old palace estate.

Hugh McIntosh had bought Marshalls (see Marshalls) in the 1820s, where he lived, and in 1828 he bought from the Crown the Manor of Havering, including all the manorial rights, which included the site of the old royal palace. McIntosh continued to lease out the land and it seems that the purchase of Bower Farm and the farm land was purely an investment. Hugh McIntosh was one of the large contractors of the Victorian era. He was responsible for building the London and Greenwich Railway, part of the East India Docks and part of the Great Western Railway. Besides his country house at Marshalls he also had a residence in Bloomsbury Square, London. He died in 1840 leaving his estates to his nephew David McIntosh. David put the Havering Park estate up for sale in 1847, but it did not sell. The next we see is that David McIntosh built in 1850 on the site of Bower Farm a new mansion which he called Havering Park. The photograph of the front of the new mansion shows that it was sited just to the west of the parish church of St John the Evangelist which means that Havering Park was built not only on the site of Bower Farm but also on the site of Havering Palace.

David McIntosh had obviously changed his mind about selling the land he had inherited at Havering-atte-Bower and after Havering Park was completed he moved in letting out Marshalls, which he had also inherited from his uncle. Mr McIntosh married in

Old garden walls of Havering Park

Havering Park

1876 and two years later he took a prominent part in the building of the new parish church which abutted his mansion. He died in 1881 aged 66 and Mrs McIntosh continued to live at Havering Park until her death in 1923. David Mcintosh was married at the age of 61 and clearly his bride was many years younger.

The house was demolished in 1925 and all that remains today are some low walls near to the parish hall in Wellington Avenue. The coach house and stable block fortunately remain and are now used as riding stables. This large building is one of only six Grade I listed buildings in the Borough.

Stables of Havering Park

## HIGH HOUSE - UPMINSTER

This large property was situated in Corbets Tey Road, Upminster, opposite St Laurence Church, and must not be confused with High House, Corbets Tey, which is still standing and a Listed Building. The house was built in 1580 and lasted over 350 years before being demolished in 1935 to make way for a shopping parade. Many alterations took place during its lifetime but it was not rebuilt and it would have been one of Upminster's oldest buildings were it still standing. As can be seen from the drawing the house was a gabled three storey building with the servants quarters at the top. The first floor boasted four bedrooms with three more on the top floor. On the ground floor there was a large entrance hall together with a dining room and a drawing room both 20 feet long. Adjacent to the house was a library which was approached by a trellis walkway together with the usual stables and outbuildings. The garden ran along the frontage to Corbets Tey Road for 300 feet and in the rear there was a four acre meadow which became the playing fields for the Junior School in St Mary's Lane.

High House was one of the major non-manor houses in Upminster and various notable people lived there from time to time. William Derham the noted scientist and Rector of St Laurence lived there from about 1690 to his death in 1735 as the Rectory had fallen into disrepair. Dr Derham was the first man to discover the speed of sound. He discovered that the sound of the guns at Woolwich took 56 seconds to reach Upminster a distance of 12 miles as the crow flies. Modern scientists, including Newton, confirmed the Doctor's figures, which were only very slightly incorrect. Dr Derham also published a work in 1696 on clock construction and the mathematics associated with this art have stood the test of time up to the present. Further information on this notable man can be found in the *History of Upminster and Cranham*.

The other notable resident at High House was Major Howard who died at the Battle of Waterloo (1815). During his time in Upminster it is said that he was visited by his friend or relative Lord Byron and that part of Byron's 'Child Harold' was written at High House.

Wilson in his *Sketches of Upminster* records that a subsequent owner of the property, Dr William Tabrum, had his coffin made prior to his death in 1865 from one of the branches of a very large cedar tree that stood in the grounds. One of the last owners was Charles Reilly, who designed Upminster Court in 1906. High House was turned into a guest house in the 1930s and on its demolition the parade of shops on the site was called Byron Parade in memory of the house's famous visitor.

High House, Upminster

Hill Place

## HILL PLACE

Hill Place stands at the top of Upminster Hill opposite the windmill and is now the Sacred Heart of Mary Girls' School. This large house was originally built in 1790 and was part of Sir James Esdaile's building programme on his Gaynes manor estate (see Gaynes Manor). In 1871 the historian Wilson says that the house was almost entirely reconstructed which is confirmed by the entry in Kelly's *Directory* of 1878, which describes the house as a modern Elizabethan style mansion standing in well-kept pleasure grounds. The house is built of red brick with stone dressings with an assortment of mullioned and projecting windows. The chimneys are very large and mock Tudor. The principal rooms were very grand with the vestibule and hall being both paved with marble and the walls lined with carved oak panelling. The dining room was 27 feet by 22 feet and 14 feet high. The fireplace mantel was surrounded in handsomely carved marble and stone. The drawing room was 30 feet by 27 feet and similarly finished. The ground floor also contained a library, morning room and boudoir. The staircase is of carved oak leading to 15 bedrooms and bathrooms.

The grounds on the south side of St Mary's Lane covered 12 acres with a further 20 acres being on the windmill side of the road which were formerly part of the mill property. A tenant of the property in the 19th century was Miss Ellen Willmott, the well-known horticulturist, later of Warley Place, who transformed the 20 acres on the other side of the road into an ornamental well wooded paddock. She planted trees and shrubs in abundance and the end result placed the house and grounds `in a distinguished position among the residential homes in the neighbourhood'.

Notable owners include Major E S Woodiwiss, who kept a private zoo in the grounds and who had the honour of welcoming to his house W G Grace, the cricketer, when he visited Upminster in 1896. The zoo buildings included various stables, three aviaries, an eyrie and a bear pit. There is a story that when a visitor was charged at by an alpaca he threw his new top hat at the animal who promptly stopped and ate the hat. A subsequent owner in 1899 was Sir E P Wills, of the tobacco family, who the same year bought Bridge House farm at the bottom of Upminster Hill, roughly where Bridge Avenue is today. In 1927 Hill Place became the Convent Collegiate School a boarding and day school for girls of all ages and for boys up to 8 years. A new wing was added in 1930 and the chapel was built in 1935. At the outbreak of war in 1939 the school closed and was transferred as a complete unit to Chilton House, Buckinghamshire. During the war the Army occupied the school; on the cessation of hostilities the school reopened in 1946 and is now a day school for girls.

## HORNCHURCH HALL

Hornchurch Hall was sited on the corner of Inskip Drive and High Street, right next door to The Chaplaincy. Hornchurch Hall was a manor and with Suttons manor formed the original endowment by Henry II of Hornchurch Priory in the 12th century. It is believed that the Priory stood on the site of the Chaplaincy (*q.v.*). The Priory was dissolved in 1391 with the Hornchurch estates being sold to William of Wykeham, Bishop of Winchester who gave the manors to New College, Oxford.

From 1400 it seems that the old Priory building or the new Chaplaincy extended into the building which was eventually known as Hornchurch Hall. In the 15th century the two buildings were divided by a wall and New College leased out the manor, which was a rectory manor, entitling the lessee to collect tithes. In 1663 the estate comprised 306 acres falling slightly to 280 acres by 1849. Hornchurch Hall was described as a 16th century house with a 17th century chimney with a large late 18th or early 19th century addition to the south front. Unfortunately the house was damaged by bombing in 1940 and was demolished in 1941. The manor was reputed to have the largest genuine tithe barn in Essex, which burnt down in a fire in 1859. A new barn was built which was also very large and it was this latter barn that was used for church services during the restoration of the church in 1870-1.

## HORNCHURCH CHAPLAINCY

Although there is a separate section in this work for Rectories and Vicarages, I am giving the old Chaplaincy at Hornchurch an entry to itself as it is a little different from the other houses for the clergy. When William of Wykeham endowed various lands in Hornchurch to New College, Oxford, in the 1390s, this transfer included the right to appoint a person to the living at St Andrews, Hornchurch. The deed of his presentation to the living described him not as a Vicar or Rector, but as a Chaplain and Vicar Temporal. The properties that have stood on the site were not owned by the church but by New College which distinguishes this building from the usual rectory or vicarage.

The Chaplaincy stood behind the high wall of the house, which still stands, opposite St Andrew's church where Chaplaincy Gardens is now. There have been houses on the site since the 14th century with the last house being a mixture of periods. This last house appeared to be mainly Victorian, but included evidence of earlier periods. The house was of no architectural or historical interest and consequently planning permission for housing development was not opposed. The land was sold to a builder in 1969, but before demolition in 1970 the Hornchurch Historical Society were given permission to photograph the building. It was discovered that under wall panels in the upstairs rooms were walls of wattle and daub construction indicating that the house was much older than everyone thought. At that stage a date of late 14th or early 15th century was suggested. Unfortunately a fire damaged much of the building, but it was possible to rescue an undamaged wall which was cut into sections and taken away for further examination. At present the wall is with the Passmore Edwards Museum, but is among items that are expected to figure in a Borough Museum at some time.

Subsequent investigation has established that the wall is dated about 1400 and was at the western end of the Chaplaincy with the remainder of the building being of 16th,18th and the 19th century construction. It appears that the wall has always been an interior wall which is why it has survived so long. The construction was timber framed with upright rough hewn laths between the main timbers with cross lathes tied with pliable twigs. The whole was covered with daubs of chopped straw and mud with the surface being faced with plaster at a later date. What makes this discovery that much interesting is that the site of Hornchurch Priory has never been found and it is quite possible that this building right opposite the church is the location. The Priory was established by Henry II in the 12th century and, although dissolved in 1391, it is known that a house was built on the Priory site in about 1400.

# LANGTONS

Langtons is off Billet Lane, Hornchurch, and the house, in the care of the London Borough of Havering, was built about 1760 in the typical Georgian style of the day. The building is dated by a pump which stood in a bath house in the gardens which bore the date 1760 and the initials 'J.M.' which probably refer to John Massu who lived at Langtons until his death in 1807. The Massu family were Huguenot refugees who became wealthy silk merchants in the City of London. John Massu died at an early age and his wife continued to live in the house until she died in 1850. Another notable owner of the property was Colonel Henry Holmes who bought the house in 1891, although he did not live there himself as he also owned Grey Towers, where he resided from 1876 until his death in 1913.

The last family to own Langtons were the Williams, with the daughter marrying Arthur Parks, who continued to live at the house until 1929; following the death of her husband. In this year she gave the house and grounds to the Hornchurch Urban District Council for use as their offices on the condition that the gardens are open to the public and that the house is kept in the same condition as when she lived there. Elizabeth Parks died in 1968 at the age of 86 and was buried at St Andrew's, Hornchurch. The house is today the local Registrar's office and it is pleasing to record that the local authority have kept their promise to Elizabeth Parks and there is a fine Georgian house in our midst with a well kept lake and gardens.

Langtons stable block

Langtons orangery

# LAURIE HALL

Laurie Hall was sited at the eastern end of Romford Market near where the pedestrian underpass is located. Mr John Laurie came to live at Marshalls in about 1847, having already had a distinguish career in London with an interest in the law and the rehabilitation of discharged prisoners. Soon after arriving in Romford he became a Justice of the Peace for the 'Liberty' and was also a Magistrate. These offices brought to his attention the lack of space at the present Court House and he promoted a plan to develop the eastern end of Romford into a new residential area to include a new court house which soon acquired the name of Laurie Town. The eastern end of the market was a deserted area which had previously been used as brickfields and also where there was an objectionable pond called Loam Pond sited roughly where the underpass is today. The plan was to buy up this land together with other land on either side of Main Road towards Gidea Park building a new County Court at the top of the market and smart houses leading away from Romford.

The County Court building was completed in 1853 and, as can be seen from the photograph of 1905, the architect chose the Greco-Roman style for this edifice. The building was never used as a court and through its life of just over 100 years it took on many rôles. Apart from a square of pleasant Victorian villas adjacent to the new hall the project did not get off the ground as John Laurie was not able to purchase further land for building purposes. The scheme died with Mr Laurie in 1865 and the building was first used for entertainments on the ground floor and the Liberty Institute was upstairs. The property went through a period of disuse, but was then renovated and used as a wine and spirit store and offices for the market cattle salesmen. Later a builders' merchant moved in downstairs, with the upper floor being used by the Catholic Apostolic Church and later by the Romford Town Mission. The 1905 photograph has the words WE PREACH CHRIST painted under the pediment. The biggest change to the building and its most prolific period was when it was converted into Romford's first cinema in 1913, being one of the first in the country.

After closure as a cinema Laurie Hall had various minor uses, but its heyday had passed and eventually it was rather a white elephant, although the photograph dated about 1950, showing the side of the building and the War Memorial (now moved), evidences that this large building was still structurally sound. The villas were pulled down in 1964/68 to make way for the Central Library and Laurie Hall itself disappeared in early 1970.

Laurie Hall and toll gate

Laurie Town houses,
War Memorial, Mile post and
Park End Road

War Memorial and Laurie Hall

Demolition (*photograph from Ian Wilkes collection*)

76

## LEE GARDENS and WYCH ELM

These two properties are linked for, although their histories cover differing periods, both estates covered similar land in Wingletye Lane, Hornchurch. The older of the two is Lee Gardens which dates back to the 13th century and was one of the original twelve manors that existed in Hornchurch in the Middle Ages. This manor stretched the whole length of Wingletye Lane from the Southend Arterial Road in the north to the Upminster Road in the south. Through the centuries Lee Gardens was always an important estate in this part of Hornchurch and is mentioned by name on maps dated 1594 and 1771 with other large houses in the area like Nelmes and Lilliputs. By 1869 the estate was down to only 112 acres and as the house was now beyond repair it was demolished and a small farmhouse was built, but this was demolished in 1919 to make way for residential development. Most of the land comprising the residue of the estate was latterly being worked by the neighbouring Lilliputs farm. Old maps show the site of the original house as being roughly where Rayburn Road is located today off Wingletye Lane. Wych Elm farm stood where Wych Elm Road is today off Wingletye Lane. The land formed part of the Lee Gardens manor and the farm took its name from a magnificent wych elm tree, of abnormal proportions, which once stood in front of the house. The house was 18th century and as the photograph shows it was an attractive three bay two storey building with attics.

Wych Elm Farm

## LILLIPUTS

The Chapman and André map of Essex of 1777 mentions Lilliputs by name and, considering only about twelve properties in Hornchurch are accorded this honour, this gives some indication of the importance of this farm. Like Dury Falls (see Dury Falls) Lilliputs was originally all part of the Middle Ages manor of Lees Gardens, which stretched the length of Wingletye Lane. Lilliputs is still standing and can be found at the end of a chase leading off Wingletye Lane, near Wych Elm Road. Wingletye Lane was originally called Hay Street and the small area at the entrance to Lilliputs is still called Hay Green.

The present house is a timber framed 17th century building, encased in brick in the early 18th century. There is evidence of a moat which indicates that earlier properties stood on the site. A property called Mayland, alias Drywoods, in the Lane can be traced back to 1345 and it does seem that this Middle Ages property occupied the same site as Lilliputs today. The Bearblock family had strong connections with Hornchurch with Mr Peter Esdaile Bearblock residing at Lilliputs during the first half of the 19th century. He was a Captain in the 15th Essex Rifles and, during his time at Lilliputs, the shooting range for the soldiers was in a meadow adjoining the house.

# MARKS

There has been much discussion through the centuries as to whether Marks was sited within the then Liberty of Havering or within the parish of Dagenham. The confusion is not in respect of where the actual house was sited but in which administrative district the property fell. The house was right on the Havering/Dagenham boundary in Whalebone Lane, just north of the Eastern Avenue (A12) on land that is now Warren Farm. The records show that rent was paid both to the manor of Havering (Havering Palace) and also to the manor of Barking. In the 15th century, at the time the Liberty of Havering was created in 1465, it seems that the incumbent of Marks, Thomas Urswick, had the Dagenham/Havering boundary altered so that Marks came within the new Liberty of Havering. Urswick was a prominent lawyer and, as he lived on one of the boundaries of the new Liberty, it is quite likely that he used his influence and position to ensure that his property came within the boundary. He would then have enjoyed the privileges of living within the Liberty, one of which would be of taking deer from the royal forest.

Thomas Urswick built a new house on the moated site some time between 1465 and 1470. His inventory of 1479 records the property as having 20 rooms, together with a bakehouse, a dairy and a chapel. It does seem that Urswick's house changed very little for nearly 350 years until it was demolished in 1808. The drawing, copied from one done by Lysons in 1796, shows a quadrangled property surrounded by a moat with embattled towers at two corners. A bridge crossed the moat from the south end. The history of the manor probably dates back a hundred years or so before Urswick built his magnificent house, as reference is made to Marks being part of Barking manor in the 14th century, although some historians think that the manor existed at the time of the Norman Conquest.

Not many manors had the right to have their own manor court, but Marks seems to have had this privilege from the 14th century. When local authorities came into being, coupled with a more sophisticated legal system, the rather feudal system whereby tenants were brought before their lord of the manor to be tried for their misdoings fell by the wayside. In addition to its own manor court Marks had the right to 'estovers' which was the right to take certain game from Hainault Forest and also to take wood from the forest.

Through the centuries the manor grew in size peaking at 460 acres in the late 15th century. This was not especially large for such an important manor, but what the estate lacked in size seems to have been made up in style. The Mildmay family had a long association with the house and one Caren Hervey Mildmay (1690-1784), Member of Parliament for Harwich and also private secretary to Viscount Bolingbroke, kept a large household and entertained in the grand tradition. General Oglethorpe of Cranham Hall, (*q.v.*) occasionally dined with Mildmay at Marks and said that he likened the occasion to what England was like in centuries past, referring presumably to the old house and the hospitality. It is also recorded that it was not unusual to see six coaches full of Mildmay's weekend guests being taken to attend church at St Edward's in the Market Place.

A previous Mildmay with the same name commanded a Parliamentary regiment during the Civil War. The Royalists were on their way from London through Essex to Chelmsford and Colchester and obviously their route through Romford took them close to the Mildmay estate. They chose to attack this stronghold in June, 1648, and it is said that Mildmay had to make his escape by swimming across the moat. He was later pardoned by the King and his effigy is on his tomb in St Edward's church.

Earlier still, it is interesting to see that when Sir George Hervey, who held Marks, died in 1605 there was an Inquest, not to enquire into the cause of death, but to investigate to whom Sir George was leaving his estate. The reason being that the King, on whose land Marks stood, wished to know what was happening to the land. As it happened, the estate passed to the son with other bequests to Sir George's wife. Presumably the King could overturn a bequest if he felt that his land was not passing to someone suitable. In addition to Marks Sir George Hervey also held a house and 30 acres in Orsett, 40 acres in Horndon, 20 acres of marsh at Woolwich and Copped Hall or Copthall in Dagenham, together many other small tenements and pieces of land in the area.

Marks had its heyday from the 16th to the 18th century, but it seems that during the latter part of the century the estate was gradually broken up and the house was demolished in 1808 after many years of decay and neglect.

# MARSHALLS

The house stood just to the west of Havering Drive and to the north of Park Drive, where two junior schools are now. The estate in its heyday accounted for all the land between Eastern Avenue and Main Road north/south, and Pettits Lane and North Street east/west. Nikolaus Pevsner, in his survey of Essex houses, described it as a house with 'a stuccoed Georgian five bay front (a tuscan porch) and earlier gabled back parts'.

The illustration is a copy of a drawing done in 1890 when the property was probably in its prime. The bridge in the picture still exists. The house is by no means a stately home and can best be described as a gentleman's residence. In a sale catalogue of 1816 it showed that the grounds contained much water stocked with fish. The house itself had on the ground floor a front dining room which was 23 feet by 20 feet and another dining room 23 by 19 feet 6 inches. Also on the ground floor was a library. The first floor had five bedrooms and various closets with seven further rooms on the third floor which were probably used by the servants. The rear rooms on the ground floor included the kitchens and the house-keepers room together with the servants hall and various rooms used as a dairy, bakehouse, ale and wine cellars. The name of the house appears to have been taken from a family of that name that featured in many local records of the 12th century onwards. The Thorowgood family owned the property from 1618 when the estate was only 40 acres until the early 18th century. When the estate was sold in 1816 there were 112 acres and it was acquired by Rowland Stephenson. Mr Stephenson became well known for two reasons. Firstly, because of the large parties he held at the house and, secondly, due to the fraud he perpetrated against the bank called Remington, Stephenson & Co., of which he was a partner. His parties were often gaming parties and maybe he had to defraud the bank to make up his losses. After the bank failed the losses were said to be half a million pounds - which, of course, was worth much more in those days. Stephenson was made bankrupt and it is interesting to note that he was also the Member of Parliament for Leominster.

In 1829 the house and estate was purchased by Hugh McIntosh who had bought the Manor of Havering estate a year earlier (see Havering Palace). The estate continued with the McIntosh family until 1924, when it was all put up for sale. The parkland was all developed into housing estates although the house and stables remained. The stables were used as a riding school with the house being used as the Conservative Club until after World War II. The house was next used as an annex to the Romford County Technical School. With new school buildings being erected, the house deteriorated and it was demolished in December, 1959.

Marshalls

Mawneys

82

# MAWNEYS

The manor of Mawneys dates from 1200 when King John granted `the wood at Romford' to Roger Bigod, who was the Earl of Norfolk, at a rent of five shillings a year. The manor was subordinate to the royal manor of Havering-atte-Bower. The manor house stood on a moated site only 150 yards north of High Street, Romford; the site now being occupied by the United Services Club in Mawney Road. The manor house was sometimes called Great Mawneys. In the 17th century the house was said to be of a considerable size, but by the 19th century it was an irregular shaped building which appears to have been rebuilt in the 18th century. The moat is said to have been filled in during the 1880s, but the drawing, which is from a sketch of 1888 by A B Bamford, seems to show water on at least two sides of the house.

The estate was called the manor of Romford in 1280 and it was not until the 14th century that the manor assumed the name of Mawneys, although the spelling was different, when Lord Mauny, Walter de Mauny held the estate. At that time the manor covered 140 acres. The history of the many owners of the manor can be found in the *Victoria History of Essex, Volume VII,* but the last incumbent was the Newman family who acquired the manor in 1758. Richard Newman was succeeded by his grandson, Richard Harding, who also acquired the manor of Nelmes, Hornchurch in 1781. Richard changed his name to Richard Harding-Newman in 1783. Both estates descended with the family for 100 years, with Mawneys containing 265 acres in 1846. Benjamin, who inherited the estate in 1882, had acquired very valuable land at a time when Romford was beginning to expand and being centrally situated the estate was ideal for residential development. The whole estate was sold for housing in 1883 with the 265 acres stretching from Marks Road in the south to Forest Road in the north. The house itself though lasted until 1935, when it was demolished, although for the last forty or so years of its life it was completely surrounded by houses.

Great Nelmes

Staircase. Great Nelmes

## NELMES

Nelmes was one of the twelve Hornchurch manors that existed in the Middle Ages. Its history can be traced back to the 13th and 14th centuries when Richard Elms, from whom the manor acquired its name, held about 300 acres in Hornchurch. The estate changed very little in size right up to the time the land was sold for residential development. The manor and estate became to be known as Great Nelmes and extended from the Ardleigh Green Road in the west to Wingletye Lane in the east. The site of the old mansion, which was not pulled down until 1967, was roughly where The Witherings has been built today. There is still remaining though a house known as Capel Nelmes lying 100 yards to the south-west of where Nelmes stood, which was once an outbuilding of the manor house, which was converted into a dwelling house in about 1870. This property is itself now large having had various extensions during the last few centuries with the oldest part dating from the 16th century.

The last Nelmes dated from the 16th century and originally had the traditional single storey hall which would have extended to second floor height by today's standards. Over the centuries the mansion was enlarged and it was one of only a few named houses in Hornchurch on the Chapman and André map of Essex in 1777. One of the predecessors of the rates was a hearth tax and it is recorded that Nelmes had 15 hearths in 1670, which makes it a reasonable sized house in those days. One of the most important features of the house was the main staircase dating from the 17th century, which can now be found in Capel Nelmes. It is said that this fine carved oak staircase was probably one of the best examples of the work of the Charles I period. The grounds had a walled garden and a lake and, together with an orchard and splendid cedar trees in the grounds, made Nelmes one of the finest manor houses in the area.

Of the families that lived at Nelmes, Sir William Roche was Lord Mayor of London in 1540, dying at Nelmes in 1549. Thomas Witheringe was Postmaster General to Charles I, dying on his way from Nelmes to St Andrew's Church in 1651. He has an alabaster mural monument in St Andrew's. Three generations of the Harding-Newmans lived at Nelmes in the latter part of the 18th century and it is interesting to note that this was a hunting family with fox hounds kennelled at Chelmsford and Navestock.

The 20th century saw the start of residential development with the first plots being sold in 1895. The whole estate of 241 acres was put up for sale in 1901 with only Great Nelmes, Capel Nelmes and ten acres being retained. Apart from Capel Nelmes there is still standing a tower in a front garden in Sylvan Avenue, which is a Listed Building and dated about 1650.

# MOOR HALL

Moor Hall is sited just within the Havering boundary, although the entrance today is a half mile drive off Romford Road, Aveley, in the borough of Thurrock. The historic entrance to the Hall was off Sandy Lane, also within Thurrock, which was switched to the present route due to gravel winning on part of the farm.

This rather remote farm stands 100 feet above sea level with good views of the Thames. The present house was built about the mid-18th century and it is quite clear from earlier records that there was a house on the site for a number of centuries previously. The manor house was first mentioned in 1314, when it appears that the property was all part of the Berwick manor estate. Moor Hall falls within the parish of Rainham and from parish records owners of the property have been benefactors of the church at Rainham over the centuries. A notable tenant at Moor Hall in the early 19th century was Thomas Sturgeon, who was a breeder of merino sheep, who used Rainham marshes for his grazing. Thomas Sturgeon and his family helped introduce sheep farming in other countries. In 1850 the farm had 800 acres although ten years later only 517 acres are recorded when the farm was sold to Sir Thomas Barrett Lennard of Belhus, Aveley. The farm is still substantial owning much of the land between Romford Road, Aveley, and Launders Lane, Rainham.

## NEW PLACE

The mansion called New Place was pulled down in 1924, but fortunately the stable block was saved and is now referred to as The Clockhouse. The history of the house can be traced back to 1556 when it was part of the Gaynes manor estate of Ralph Latham who also held Upminster Hall manor. This one man effectively was landlord of the whole of Upminster at that time. There is no information available on the previous houses on the site until the last one was built in 1775.

New Place mansion came into the hands of Mary Mayor on the death of her aunt, Mrs John Mayor. Mary married Mr James Esdaile, as he was then, in 1748 and they lived at New Place. Subsequently James Esdaile was knighted and rebuilt New Place in 1775 having bought Gaynes manor a few years earlier. He continued with his rebuilding programme which included Gaynes and other houses in Upminster. New Place had then come back into the lordship of Gaynes manor with other members of the Esdaile family living at New Place when Sir James moved into his newly built Gaynes mansion (see Gaynes manor). New Place was eventually occupied by Sir James's son James. This James had seven children but, tragically, two sons died within a week of each other at the ages of 20 and 19 in May 1802. The third death was one of his daughters, Susanna, who died three years later at the age of eighteen. These family deaths obviously had a lasting effect on James Esdaile for, in 1812, he was found shot in the grounds of New Place whilst his carriage was being brought to the front door for a business trip to London. There seems little doubt that it was suicide brought about through grief for his family losses although the records are silent on the cause of death.

The New Place which James's father had built was of red brick and quadrangular in shape having east and west wings. In the front there was a flight of stone steps under a Gothic portico leading to the main entrance. The east wing was rebuilt and enlarged in 1870. Adjacent to the house was a large stable block over which was erected a large clock which was brought from the arsenal at Woolwich. There being no other public clock in the village at that time it was referred to as the village clock and in fact in later years the house itself came to be known as the Clock House. The gardens of the mansion also remain as public gardens which include a moat which was immediately behind the old house. It is not known though whether previous houses were in fact erected within the moat, but this is quite likely.

New Place was never a large estate in the context of the big country houses of the 18th and 19th centuries having only about 65 acres of land which extended from the major crossroads in Upminster to where Argyle Gardens is today, which was the parish boundary with Cranham. The fields extended back to about Springfield Gardens. It is interesting to note that when the Esdaile or subsequent families went to church at St Laurence's they used a shrubbery walk which went just inside their boundary in St Mary's Lane all the way to the Bell Inn, round the public house still within their grounds and out by way of a gate which was right opposite the church entrance. That gateway in Corbets Tey Road is still there and forms one of the entrances to the Upminster Junior School. The effect of this

New Place

New Place stable block (The Clock House)

private walkway was that occupiers of New Place did not have to use the public roads which were quite atrocious in those days.

New Place was sold by the Esdaile family in 1839 to James Harmer, an Alderman of the City of London. Mr Harmer was the proprietor of the *Weekly Dispatch* newspaper, which was only inferior to *The Times* at that time. The *Dispatch* published a series of articles which had the effect of preventing a candidate being elected at Southwark. When the time came for James Harmer to be elected as Lord Mayor, *The Times* retaliated, denouncing Harmer's newspaper as an `infidel paper''. This campaign had the desired effect and James Harmer was rejected by the City and resigned as an Alderman.

As Upminster developed in the 20th century, New Place and its 65 acres was sold to a local builder in 1909 for residential development. New Place was let as there was no immediate need to pull the house down as there was not yet the demand for new houses in that part of Upminster. Development at that time was taking place around the railway station.

Upminster's population was growing and there was talk of buying a building to use as council offices. Up till then meetings had taken place in a local school. There was objection from the residents who did not feel that a parish council, with its limited powers, needed a Town Hall as it was now being called. The 1914-18 War pushed the matter into the background but by the time it was resurrected again in 1922 Upminster's population had grown some more. The builder owner of New Place, W P Griggs, was now ready to pull down both the house and the stable block and so the parish council put forward a plan to buy either both buildings for £3,000 or just the stable block for £1,800, both schemes to include the immediate gardens of the house. The electorate opted for the cheaper scheme which went ahead with a loan of £2,000 from Essex County Council to cover conversion costs. The parish council used The Clockhouse as their offices for ten years, until the parish became part of Hornchurch Urban District Council in 1934. During this period the building was also used as the parish fire station. After 1934 the building was converted into a public library and ambulance garage and remained as such until 1963. Following a period when the building remained empty the old stable block has now been converted into a residential home.

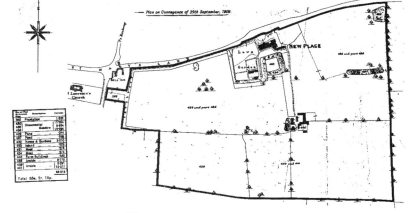

# NORTH OCKENDON HALL

Comparisons can be made between Cranham and North Ockendon as two of the smaller parishes in the Borough, whose growth was almost identical in earlier years. Both parishes had a population of about 150 in 1670 rising to 240 and about 340 in 1801 and 1851 respectively. They both had a manor house adjacent to the parish church with histories going back to the Domesday Book. There the comparison ends for, whilst Cranham continued to grow with its population explosion in the 20th century, North Ockendon's numbers fell to only 291 in 1931. Nevertheless the principal manor house, North Ockendon Hall, continued to be the focus of this parish's community and had it not been damaged by bombing during the 1939-45 War then, like Cranham Hall, it may still have been standing today.

It is probably fortunate that London's suburban sprawl did not extend to North Ockendon as the site of the Hall is still easily identifiable. North Ockendon Hall lay within a moat just south of the St Mary Magdalene Church. If one walks down Church Road past the church the moat is still quite visible and in fact has been cleaned out to improve the fishing which now takes place. Several garden walls remain which are now Listed Buildings and although a couple of bungalows have been built on the manor house site it is easy to imagine what this rural manor house looked like.

The Domesday Book of 1086 mentions two manors in North Ockendon which were both held by Westminster Abbey after William the Conqueror came to the throne. Successive manor houses are not always built on exactly the same site, but in North Ockendon's case it does seem that they were always built within the moat which probably dates back to the Middle Ages. The last house on the site was of 16th century origin of red brick with additions in the early 18th and 19th centuries. The photographs give a good idea of its shape and size and it is a pity that it was not renovated after the War.

The Poyntz family were connected with North Ockendon Hall from the 14th century when Poyntz Poyntz married into the Baldwin family who held the manor at that time. The manor passed from one Poyntz to another right up till the 17th century. The most notable was Sir Gabriel Poyntz, who left his mark on the chapel in the parish church, where successive lords of the manor have been buried. He commissioned sculptures to be created of his ancestors in stone which appear as eight `portraits' of the husbands and wives kneeling and facing each other with a stool between. Another notable owner of the manor in the early 1700s  was Sir Thomas Littleton Bt., who was speaker of the House of Commons and later Treasurer of the Navy. The Benyon family bought the manor in 1758 with Richard Benyon already owning manors in Ilford and Gidea Hall, Romford. In 1937 the Hall was sold by the Benyon family to pay death duties.

PUBLIC HOUSES

Within the Borough of Havering there are only five public houses that are Listed buildings, although only four are these have always been hostelries, as the Morris Dancer in Melksham Close, Harold Hill, was previously called New Hall and was a farmhouse until the Harold Hill estate was built and its use changed. Reference is made to the history of the Morris Dancer/New Hall under Dagnams.

The other four Listed public houses are:-

Golden Lion, High Street, Romford
King's Head, High Street, Hornchurch
The Lamb, Market Place, Romford
The Ship, Main Road, Gidea Park

A whole book could be written on the inns both past and present within the Borough, but I will, for the purposes of this book, just mention a few that have interesting snippets of history relating to them. Romford has always had more than an average number of public houses due to its situation as a main trunk route to East Anglia. In 1686 there were inns in the town capable of providing 139 beds and stabling for 404 horses. There were a further 18 beds in Hare Street (Main Road), Gidea Park, and stables for 38 horses. A survey in 1762 revealed 22 licensed inns in Romford and a further three at Hare Street. Romford's *Classified Directory* of 1811 records 19 inns, falling to 18 in 1823/24. There were at least this number right up to the 1930s.

Of all the Romford inns only the Golden Lion remains in an historic building with The Lamb, which dates back to 1681, now housed in a building rebuilt in 1852-3. The Cock and Bell inn in the Market Place is still standing, but is now The Church House (*q.v*). The Golden Lion is referred to in the will of Roger Reede in 1482, when is was known as The Lion. It was not until the 17th century that it became the Golden Lion. At that time the pub owned 4 acres of meadow near Havering Well (now the small graveyard at Roneo Corner) in Romford. Records show that the inn was invariably leased out to tenants, with the lease of 1791 listing the property as having attached to it yards, gardens, coach houses, stables and brew houses. In the 19th century the upper floors comprised 9 bedrooms and 3 sitting rooms, with the ground floor having a coffee room, bar, two parlours, store room and kitchen. Outside there was a carriage house capable of housing 4 carriages, four loose stables which could take 10 horses each and an ostlers cottage. The meadow is mentioned again and is described as being 'on the west side of the road to Havering Well in the parish of Hornchurch'. Ind & Co became tenants in the mid-19th century.

The Golden Lion looks today like two distinct buildings with its square three storey frontage to the High Street and the lower jettied frontage to North Street. In fact, the building is made up of three sections, all timber framed, dating from the early 16th to the early 17th century. The jettied east side at one time extended to the front, but in the 18th century the High Street frontage was raised by one storey and faced in brick. The three

The Ship, Gidea Park

The Lamb, Romford Market

The Golden Lion, Romford

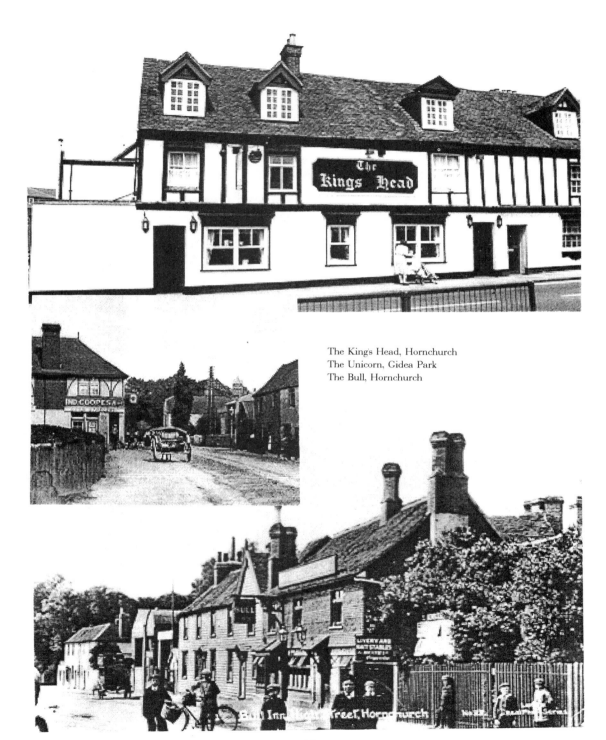

The King's Head, Hornchurch
The Unicorn, Gidea Park
The Bull, Hornchurch

94

storey block was then given a cement rendering in 1880. Of the many public houses to be found in the Market Place or the High Street none can be traced as far back as the Golden Lion, although there are references to named inns dating from later in the 15th century, details of which can be found in other works of reference.

In 1762 the Ship and the Unicorn were to be found in Hare Street, now Main Road, Gidea Park, although there are no records of the third inn at this location. The Unicorn was rebuilt in Tudor style in the 1930s, although its name has now been changed. The photograph of the early 1900s shows the previous building almost on the road frontage and obliterating the Ship, almost next door. The cottages opposite are still standing and Listed (see Listed Cottages). The Ship dates from the late 16th or early 17th century, although with many alterations. It is interesting to note that the survey of 1762 also recorded 5 inns at Collier Row and 3 at Noak Hill, the oldest survivor being the Bear, Noak Hill Road. This public house was previously called the Goat, but changed its name in 1715.

The oldest building at Havering-atte-Bower is Blue Boar Hall which, as its name suggests, was once an inn. The house, at the top of Orange Tree Hill opposite the village green, is recorded as having a license in 1712, but this seems to have lapsed by the time of the 1762 survey. Both the Royal Oak and the Orange Tree at Havering-atte-Bower have long histories, although both are now housed in relatively modern public houses.

In 1762 Hornchurch had 8 inns, of which 4 were in the village centre. By the mid-19th century there were 9 in the centre and 5 in the countryside. The King's Head is the only one still housed in an ancient building and, although there have been many alterations through the centuries, this inn dates back to 1680. The building is timber framed and was owned by the Hornchurch Brewery on the opposite side of the road, before being purchased by Mann Crossman & Paulin in 1925. The rear of the premises was used by the tanning industry which thrived in Hornchurch and subsequently there was a quoit ground in the back yard. The Bull and the White Hart (both sadly re-named) in the High Street are both inns with a long history, with the former dating back to the 16th century and although we do not know long the old White Hart has been in existence it is probably of a similar age to the Bull. Both are now housed in relatively modern buildings, with the White Hart having been rebuilt twice since it was burnt down in 1872. The Harrow, Hornchurch Road, is also over a century old having been rebuilt in 1894. The Crown, at the Romford end of the Hornchurch Road, is said to date from 1433, but was rebuilt in the 1920s. The Albion at Dovers Corner roundabout (previously called The Canteen) would seem to have been built in an area where there was little population in 1880, but it appears that the inn was built to serve the London Rifle Brigade volunteers whose rifle range was near by.

Compared with Romford and Hornchurch, Upminster has always had a much smaller population, but there was still a good sprinkling of inns covering the Upminster, Corbets

The Angel, Rainham

The Phoenix, Rainham

The Canteen - now the Albion - Rainham

Tey and Hacton area. Upminster village had the Bell and the Masons' Arms, with a further three inns at Corbets Tey and two in the hamlet of Hacton. Only the Masons' Arms and the Huntsman & Hounds remain, both having been rebuilt in 1928 and 1896 respectively. The population of Upminster in the 19th century was only about 1,300 people (260 houses) and it is difficult to see how so many inns could support such a small catchment area. With the absence of transport and entertainment the local pub was all that there was available for the community to while away their free time. All older Upminster residents regret the passing of the Bell inn, sited at the central crossroads. This inn is said to have been in existence prior to 1636, although the last building on the site was built in the 18th century.

Cranham supported just one inn prior to its modern development - the Plough in Front Lane, about a quarter of a mile from its new location in the centre of the shopping area.

North Ockendon had a population of just 250 people in the early 1800s, which supported the one inn in the village, namely the White Horse. This inn is still there with the population little changed as we near the 21st century.

The three public houses in central Rainham are all rebuilds of previous inns on the same site. The oldest building is the Phoenix, rebuilt in 1891. This inn was a post house in the 1820/30s before new premises were found in Upminster Road South. The Angel was rebuilt in 1907 with the photograph showing how it looked previously. Incidentally, the 1905 photograph of the Phoenix shows it little changed from today except that the balcony has now been taken down. The present Bell is a modern building, although this inn dates back to at least 1718 and probably earlier. The Angel and the Phoenix were also in existence in the early 18th century.

At the end of Ferry Lane, Rainham where the road meets the Thames there has always been a small community until recent times. This was due not to the industrial area we know today, but because of the ferry that plied across the river to Kent from the jetty at the end of Ferry Lane, where goods were also shipped. The jetty was also used as a stopping point for paddle-steamers that plied between London and Ramsgate in the 19th century. At one time there was a community numbering 200, served by the Three Crowns inn, sited right on the river frontage as the 1931 photograph shows. Records can trace the existence of the inn back as far as 1556. Before 1772 the inn was known as The French Horn. The last building was erected in the 1830s. Following the industrialisation of Ferry Lane the population fell and by 1940 only one family remained, apart from the publican. The Three Crowns finally closed in 1951 and was demolished in 1972, with part of the ground floor being incorporated in factory premises.

I have concluded with a selection of photographs of public houses that still remain today, although most have been altered somewhat, with one or two having changed their name.

The Bell, Upminster

The Plough, Cranham

The Bell, Collier Row

Collier Row, Romford.

98

The White Hart, Collier Row

The Three Crowns, Rainham Ferry

The Bridge House, Upminster

The Squirrel's Head, Squirrels Heath

The Drill, Squirrels Heath

The Masons' Arms, Upminster

The Cricketers', Hornchurch

The White Hart, Romford

The Coopers' Arms, Rush Green

## PYRGO PARK

Pyrgo Park occupied a large tract of land in the northern part of the Borough between Broxhill Road and North Road, Havering-atte-Bower up to the boundary with Stapleford Abbots. Mansions within the park have been approached by two long drives either from the South Lodge in Broxhill Road or from North Lodge in North Road. At its peak in 1919 the estate comprised 824 acres.

The history of Pyrgo goes back to the 15th century and there are occasional references to the house being subsequently used as a dower house for the queens of England on the death of the king. There is no doubt that Pyrgo formed part of the royal manor of Havering Palace when it was acquired by Henry VIII in 1541, but there are no definite records that the house was ever used as a dower house. There are references though to the house being the residence for a time of Princess Mary (daughter of Henry VIII) in 1538, but it was not a royal household at that time. Henry did stay there himself in 1543 when he held a meeting of his Council at Pyrgo. By 1558 the estate was back in private hands as Elizabeth I, on her accession, granted Pyrgo to Lord John Grey, uncle of Lady Jane Grey, who had been Queen of England for only nine days. Maybe Elizabeth made this gesture to the Grey family as some recompense for the tragedy that befell Lady Jane, who lost her head after such a short time on the throne. Queen Elizabeth visited Lord John on her Progress of 1561, although all the members of the Grey family were not in favour with the queen. In Henry VIII's will Lady Jane Grey's sister, Catherine, was to be the next heir to the throne and although Edward VI and Mary had occupied the throne subsequently, for a total of only 11 years, Elizabeth still saw Lady Catherine Grey as a threat. Lady Catherine incurred the queen's displeasure by becoming secretly married and so Catherine and her husband were both committed to the Tower of London. Because of the plague in London in 1563, Lady Catherine was sent to her uncle at Pyrgo and placed in his custody to remain there 'at Her Majesty's pleasure'. The couple were separated and Lady Catherine did not obtain her freedom before she died. Lord John had his own chapel at Pyrgo in which he was buried although all the tombs were removed to Havering church in about 1770, with the chapel being pulled down a few years later.

By 1814 the whole of the 16th century house had been demolished, with successive owners living in the adjacent farmhouse. Robert Field pulled down the farmhouse to build a new Pyrgo on the site in 1852 and this was enlarged in 1862 to be described as a mansion in 'Classical Italian' style faced with Suffolk white bricks with dressings and columns of Portland stone. The grounds were later landscaped with Victorian gardens and a lake, with the estate being described in 1867 in a sale catalogue as fit for "a gentleman of rank and wealth, or for a merchant prince". At that time the house had its own gas works and it is also noted that a new chapel was built a short way from the house. The house was demolished in 1940 and it seems that no family held the estate for very long in the 20th century - probably due to the cost in maintaining such a large property. All that remains today are the two lodges at the north and south ends of the estate, together with the drive from the south lodge which now goes to the old stable block and Home Farm close to the site of the house.

Many old house have stories associated with them about secret passages and tunnels and Pyrgo is no exception. The story goes that in 1860 the Rev. John Aitken wished to investigate a subterranean passage, said to exist in the grounds of Pyrgo Park. Probably with the rebuilding of Pyrgo a few years earlier the passage way had been uncovered. The entrance was found near the ice-house, itself an underground structure used for storing ice and as a cold room centuries ago. With James Newland, a principal Havering parishioner, they proceeded in a south-westerly direction through an arched passageway and, despite the problems of foul air, eventually exited near to the Vicarage which is opposite the village green. If one looks on a map the distance from the site of Pyrgo to the Vicarage is about half a mile. More interesting is that if this line is extended further south-west it meets the site of the former Havering Palace and one wonders if this tunnel was originally built as an escape route for royal visitors should the crown be in peril at some time.

Another feature to be seen on a map of the area is that the shortest route to Stapleford Abbots and beyond from Broxhill Road is directly across Pyrgo Park via the track between the south and north lodges. It seems that in the early 1800s this route was used by local residents and tradespeople to avoid the circuitous route through Havering-atte-Bower village. Landowners at this time were enclosing common land and like Upper Bedfords this occasionally extended to roads. The `road' across Pyrgo Park was closed in the early 19th century with the owner contending that it was `a private road and only open to the public by courtesy'. There seems to have been proof that it was a public road but when the time came to produce the evidence the principal spokesman failed to appear. Consequently the drive became a private road but fortunately the route of the drive is now a public footpath enabling local residents to enjoy this old royal park. Another public footpath across the park leads from North Road, fairly close to the Vicarage, across the fields to the site of the mansion. This walk gives some idea of the length of the underground passage mentioned above, the story of which seems to be factual.

## RAILWAY STATIONS

The map shows there are nine railway stations within the borough boundary and it is worth noting that nearly one hundred years separates the building of the first and the last. Romford station opened in 1839 and it was not until 1935 that Elm Park was built.

Romford was fortunate to have the railway brought to the town relatively early in the history of this form of transport. George Stephenson and his 'Rocket' and the first railway from Stockton to Darlington all happened in the 1820s, although the first passenger railway from Liverpool to Manchester was not opened until 1830. The Eastern Counties Railway Company was formed in 1834 and it was proposed to build a railway from London through Essex and into Suffolk and Norfolk terminating at Yarmouth. Work started at the London end in 1837. The engineer was Braithwaite who rented Hare Hall (Royal Liberty School) when that estate was purchased to allow to railway to pass through. It took two years to reach Romford with the first station being sited at Waterloo Road a few hundred yards west of the present site. The formal opening took place in June, 1839, with a public service commencing the following week.

In the following year, 1840, Great Gubbins farm was sold and the estate was split in two to allow the line to pass through Harold Wood. The line reached Gidea Park in 1842, although there was no station at that time, and then on to Harold Wood. The station at Harold Wood was not built for another 26 years, as the proposed housing development on the Great Gubbins farm estate had not expanded as quickly as hoped and consequently a station was not justified until 1868. Similarly, Squirrels Heath and Gidea Park station, as it was originally called, was not built until 1910 when the Gidea Hall estate was developed for housing creating a need for a station.

The railway embankment is high as the track passes through central Romford to allow for the bridges that had to be built to carry the track over Waterloo Road and South Street. A consequence of the arrival of the railway was that the high embankment which ran parallel to Victoria Road affected the performance of the windmill in Victoria Road just behind the public house (was the Rising Sun) in South Street. The windmill was pulled down in the 1870s (see Windmills).

The other railway company was the London, Tilbury and Southend Railway, formed in 1852, with the early development at Fenchurch Street and Bishopsgate and then on to Stratford, Forest Gate, Barking and thence to Tilbury with Rainham being the one station in the borough on that line, opening in 1854. From Tilbury the line was extended via Pitsea to Southend by 1856. In 1858 the line was rerouted at Bow direct to Barking cutting out the loop to Stratford and Forest Gate. Nearly thirty years later the line was straightened again by making a direct route from Barking to Pitsea through Hornchurch and Upminster.

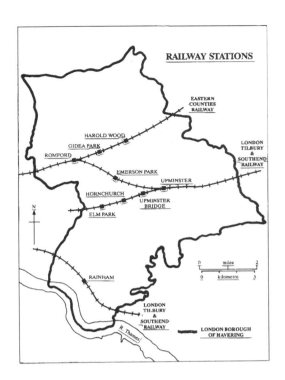

**RAILWAY STATIONS**

EASTERN COUNTIES RAILWAY

HAROLD WOOD
GIDEA PARK
ROMFORD
EMERSON PARK
UPMINSTER
HORNCHURCH
UPMINSTER BRIDGE
ELM PARK

LONDON TILBURY & SOUTHEND RAILWAY

N

RAINHAM

LONDON TILBURY & SOUTHEND RAILWAY

R. Thames

LONDON BOROUGH OF HAVERING

Romford Station

ROMFORD STATION, G.E.R.

Romford LTS Station

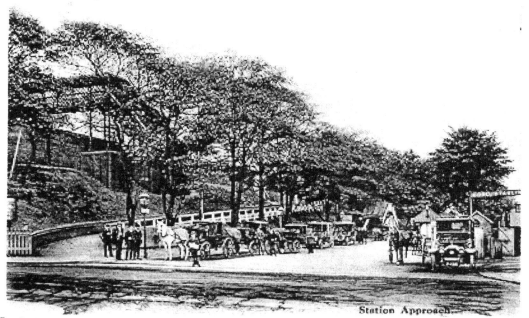

Romford GER approach

Rainham Station

Upminster Station

Hornchurch and Upminster stations were both opened in 1885. The reason for this last improvement was to free the line of Tilbury Docks freight traffic and also to improve the commuter line from Southend to London. The first turf to be cut for the Barking - Pitsea section was in fact carried out at Upminster, near the windmill on the 11th October, 1883. The line reached Pitsea to join up with the original route through Tilbury in 1888 with the direct route now reducing the journey time from Southend to London by 8 minutes.

The remaining lines in the borough were the cross-country routes from Grays to Upminster and onwards to Romford. The first section was completed in 1892 with Romford being reached a year later. The line from Grays to Romford was owned by the London, Tilbury & Southend Railway Company and came into an area owned by a competitor, the Eastern Counties Railway. Consequently, the Grays-Romford line had to have its own platform, still used today, and its own station entrance on the opposite side of South Street to the present entrance. The booking hall for the Grays line in now a retail establishment, but if one looks at the upper part, the typical railway architecture can still be seen. Emerson Park Halt was not opened until 1910 when residential development took place following the break up of the Nelmes and Lees Gardens estate.

In 1923 the Great Eastern Railway was taken over by the London & North Eastern Railway (LNER) and the London, Tilbury & Southend line by the London, Midland & Scottish railway (LMS). Electrification reached Barking by 1908, but the extension to Upminster did not take place until 1932, with Upminster Bridge station being opened on 17 December, 1934, and Elm Park on 13 May, 1935.

The LMS booking office at Romford for the branch line to Upminster was closed in 1934, following an agreement between the two railway companies although the same platform is still used.

The following chart summarises the opening dates for the nine railway stations within the present borough boundary:-

| Romford | 1839 | Hornchurch | 1885 | Gidea Park | 1910 |
| Rainham | 1854 | Upminster | 1885 | Upminster Bridge | 1934 |
| Harold Wood | 1868 | Emerson Park | 1909 | Elm Park | 1935 |

## RAINHAM HALL

Rainham Hall is next door to the parish church and one would be forgiven for assuming that this was the local manor house, which was invariably to be found in this position. The Hall though had no manorial rights and was built in 1729 by John Harle, a local businessman, who had recently moved into the area. There does not appear to have been a building on the site previously.

This early Georgian house was built in the domestic Dutch style, popular at the time and, although lacking the flamboyance of later larger Georgian mansions, it does have sufficient features to enable it to be an excellent example of the period. Internally the rooms are small and most are twelve feet by fourteen. The house originally had only three floors and a cellar with the rooms arranged quite symmetrically with two at the front and two at the back on each floor. The roof was raised in later years to accommodate six attic windows, three at the front and three at the back, which can be seen more clearly in the photograph of the rear of the house. The house is built of bricks of two colours with stone corners and with a wealth of wrought iron gates and railings both to the front and back of the house. Adjacent to the house on the other side to the church is the stable block, which is of sufficient importance to be a Listed Building, as is the Lodge which stands flush with the main road and in front of the stables and coach house. The Lodge was built a little earlier than the Hall and it is probable that John Harle lived there when his house was being built. Thereafter the Lodge was occupied by his business foreman.

John Harle came from Newcastle where he was a master mariner, shipowner and merchant. Maybe he had called at Rainham in his seafaring days as there had been a wharf in the River Ingrebourne prior to his arrival in the village. He had married a wealthy widow from Stepney at the age of thirty. With the financial backing of his wife he set up business at Rainham dredging the Ingrebourne which allowed barges to come up the river from the Thames right up to the centre of the village. He brought coal from Newcastle, softwood from Scandinavia and general building materials for the large country houses that were being built in the 18th century. There was also a demand for building materials after the Great Fire when London went through a period of expansion. Road transport over long distances was difficult in view of the poor state of the roads and with John Harle bringing all his merchandise by sea he prospered enabling him to build such a fine example of an early Georgian house which is still standing today. Apart from the attic windows the whole estate is virtually unchanged from the day it was built and we are fortunate that the house is now administered by The National Trust and open to the public at specified times. A visit is thoroughly recommended.

Iron railings at Rainham Hall
Rainham Hall
Stable block, Rainham Hall

## RAINHAM VILLAGE

It is surprising how little Rainham village centre has changed during the 20th century. The two photographs opposite were obviously taken at the same time as the horses and carts are all in the same position. The date is about 1910.

The top photograph was taken from the middle of the road in the Broadway between the church and where the library is now. The Rectory is clearly seen on the left, with the Bell public house in the background. The village shops are in the same position as today with that on the right hand end being the Post Office. The triangle in the centre of the road was known as 'The Green' and it was probably not long before the photographs were taken that this area was grass. The War Memorial with its three clock faces was erected in 1921.

The photographer changed his position for the lower view, which is on the other side of the church at the start of Upminster Road South. The Rectory is just out of the picture to the left with the first building being No. 29 The Broadway, 'Redbury', which still stands and is 18th century. This property has an interesting history as in earlier times it seems to have been associated with Redberry Wharf, which the rear of the property overlooked. On the ground floor of the house is a room, probably designed as a counting house. At the rear is brickwork that pre-dates the main structure, indicating that the house was almost rebuilt in the 18th century. Behind the house there was a large brewing copper showing that the owner of the Angel next door was a man of means if he could afford to live off the premises in a large adjacent house. The shops are seen again in the lower view this time showing the village food and hardware store which is called 'Hill - Grocer, Glass and China Stores'. The Bell pub in the top photo had been rebuilt in 1900 with the Angel having been rebuilt in 1907. Both views are postcards, one being dated 1915, and so I assume 1910 as roughly when the photographs were taken. An earlier photograph of the Angel before it was rebuilt can be found under 'Public Houses' and the Rectory is referred to under 'Rectories and Vicarages'.

Rainham Hall

112

# RECTORIES AND VICARAGES

There are some fine old buildings still standing in these categories and, although the information on each is sparse, it would be wrong to exclude them for this reason. My researches have not discovered an historic home for the incumbent at Wennington and one can only presume that as the parish was so small no house of any consequence was provided by the church. The more rural parishes have retained their Rectories or Vicarages with Romford, Hornchurch and Cranham all suffering from residential expansion and not now possessing an old property.

The 'Old Vicarage' at St Andrews, Romford adjoined the churchyard and, although it still existed in 1879, it was superseded by a large house in two acres on the west side of North Street, not very far from the Market Place. The North Street Vicarage was used until 1909, since when there has been a number of different locations. The North Street house was not demolished until 1975.

Although there are many other churches of all denominations in the Romford area none came to any prominence until the late 19th century and consequently there are no other properties of interest for other denominations.

In the case of Hornchurch, the Chaplaincy has justified a separate section in view of the historic importance of this building.

The parishes of Upminster, North Ockendon, Rainham and Havering-atte-Bower have fared much better with their rectory or vicarage still standing, although most are now used as private residences or offices.

Cranham rectory was pulled down to make way for residential development, but I have included a photograph which shows that this small parish supported a very large rectory which was seven bays wide.

In fact, most of the photographs show buildings which must rank them as almost the largest in their parish.

The clergy in centuries past was the most important person in the village, after the lord of the manor, and they enjoyed a high standard of living invariably boosted by income from tithes enabling them to support such a large property. All the properties featured were built in the 18th century and it is interesting to note the differing styles of architecture. There did not seem to be a standard style of rectory or vicarage in that century. The dates of construction for those shown are as follows:-

| Rainham | 1710 | Upminster | 1765 | Cranham | 1790 |
|---|---|---|---|---|---|
| North Ockendon | 1750 | Havering-atte-Bower | 1786 | | |

Rainham Rectory

Havering-atte-Bower Vicarage

Cranham Rectory

Upminster Rectory

North Ockendon Rectory

116

# THE ROUND HOUSE

The Round House is in Broxhill Road, at the top of the hill close to the water tower and east of the Hall (St Francis Hospice). It is only visible from the road when the trees are bare. The house was built in about 1800 by William Sheldon and is described in Pevsner's book on Essex buildings as an oval building of three storeys, plastered with eight windows on each storey. The house has four pairs of giant Tuscan pilasters, a porch of two pillars and two Ionic columns.

The story is that the house was built by a retired tea dealer in the shape of a tea caddy to commemorate how he made his fortune. The most notable occupier of the property in the early part of the 20th century was the Reverend J H Pemberton, who, besides being the incumbent of the Church of the Ascension, Collier Row, was also a well known rose grower who developed the Alexandra Rose and various other varieties, including 'Penelope' and 'Prosperity'. The Pemberton Barnes family was well known in Havering-atte-Bower with earlier members of the family owning the adjacent Hall and also the Bower House.

117

# ROMFORD GARDEN SUBURB EXHIBITION HOUSES

The majority of the land comprising the Gidea Hall estate had been transferred from the ownership of Herbert Raphael in the early 1900s (see Gidea Hall). A few new roads had been built both on the north and south sides of Hare Street, Gidea Park (now Main Road). This pleasant part of Romford was bounded on one side by the newly gifted parkland - Raphael's Park - and on the other by the Romford Golf Club, both pieces of land previously being part of the Gidea Hall estate. The central residential area was being referred to as Romford Garden Suburb and it was decided to hold an exhibition of new houses with the object being to demonstrate to planning authorities, builders and the public the up to date improvements being made in the construction industry. The object was also to influence builders to raise the standard of housing design and construction throughout the country.

The publicity brochure of 1910 said that 100 architects had contributed to the exhibition and visitors were informed that at least three visits of six hours each would be necessary to do the exhibition justice. Although the principal exhibition houses were located in the northern sector the Garden Suburb stretched all the way up Balgores Lane to the newly built Gidea Park station, which the Eastern Counties Railway Company had constructed especially for the exhibition (see Railway Stations).

The exhibition contained 140 houses, of which the majority were furnished and with their gardens landscaped. The recommended route on leaving the new station, then called Squirrels Heath and Gidea Park, was to go down Balgores Lane (9 exhibition houses) cross the main road into Heath Drive (15 houses) and from there move into Risebridge Road and Heaton Grange Road (23 and 1 respectively) and back via Reed Pond Walk (36 houses), Parkway (18), Meadway (33), into Heath Drive again and back to the station via Squirrels Heath Avenue. The refreshment centre was located at Balgores House, at the Main Road end of Balgores Lane. The journey time from Liverpool Street in 1910 was 23 minutes for a non-stop train.

As a consequence of this exhibition six houses -  43 & 64 Heath Drive, 16 & 27 Meadway, and 36 & 38 Reed Pond Walk - were, in later years, declared Listed Buildings.

16 Meadway

36 Reed Pond Walk

# SCHOOLS

If one wanted to write about every school in the Borough through all the centuries it would probably justify a whole book to itself. What I will try to do is give a picture of how education evolved in the various parishes picking out some of the historic buildings that are still standing. The big turning point in education in this country was the Education Act of 1870 by which the government assumed responsibility for seeing that all children had the opportunity to go to school which became free but compulsory. Prior to the Act the education of the young was either administered by private fee paying schools or, more commonly, by religious societies founded to provide free public education to those who wanted to learn. Prior to the Act the Church of England had founded the National School and the nonconformist churches formed the British and Foreign School Society which was generally known as the British School. The Act though did not bring any sweeping changes to the Borough as every parish had one form of school or another and the government could not afford to sweep aside the existing schools and build new ones. All it did was fill in the gaps where a school was needed with the new type of government sponsored school which had an elected school board.

There is reference to a free school in 1641, but the more important is the charity school, founded in 1711, which still survives as St Edward's Church of England primary school. This school eventually built premises and a master's house at the top of the Market where the Dolphin now stands. The school building lasted until 1926 when the premises were sold to Essex County Council, who turned it into a public library.

There was a second National School in the town, started in 1835 as the St Andrew's Church of England School. In 1843 the church built a permanent school in St Andrew's Road, where it joins London Road. The school closed in 1912 when a new school was built by the Romford Board further along London Road. A report on the school in 1910 described it as the worst school in Essex, but it is not clear if they were referring to the school building or its educational prowess. The old school building has only recently been pulled down, but the master's house is still standing and they were the oldest purpose built school buildings in the Borough.

In 1848 the British School was founded by the Congregationalists in the town. There were also National Schools at Collier Row and Noak Hill, together with a Roman Catholic school, which opened in about 1852 with 19 children. The Eastern Counties Railway Company employed many people at its tarpaulin factory in Factory Road, Squirrels Heath, with the majority living in terraced houses very close by. The Railway Company, in conjunction with the Church of England, opened a school in two terraced house in Factory Road in 1858 for children of factory workers.

When one moves away from Romford with its proliferation of schools, both private and charity, of which all cannot be mentioned, Hornchurch's situation is much more simple. There are records of small schools through the centuries, but it was the National School built next to the Chaplaincy in 1844, which was the real start of formal education in Hornchurch. The school was rebuilt in North Street in 1855, to include a teacher's house,

St Andrew's School, Romford

Dame Tipping School, Havering:
plaques of earlier buildings

Rainham School

North Street Schools, Hornchurch

Noak Hill School

St Edward's School, Romford Market

Boyd School, Cranham

123

which still stands today although the bell tower has now gone and the classroom on the corner of Westland Avenue has been replaced by a church hall. There was a charity school in South End Road, Hornchurch, in 1864, replaced by the Hornchurch Board School in Blacksmiths Lane in 1899. Harold Wood had a National School in Gubbins Lane, opened in 1886 and still standing.

Upminster was fortunate in having a National School and a British School, both opened in 1851, sited almost opposite each other in Station Road (then called Hall Lane). Before the Act of 1870 there were children of the same age being taught on opposite sides of the road due to their religious backgrounds. With the passing of the Act a School Board was formed with the schools being amalgamated - with boys going to the National School and the girls to the British School. The two ex-church schools worked in reasonable harmony until a new school was built in St Mary's Lane in 1928. The British School was pulled down in 1936, but the National School lasted until the late 1960s (site of Nat West Bank).

The small parish of Havering-atte-Bower was fortunate in having a school for poor children, built by Lady Tipping of Pyrgo Park in 1724, and this was sited on the village green. The photograph shows the original plaque, which says that Lady (Dame) Anne Tipping erected and endowed the school with £10 a year the money coming from the Pyrgo estate. Dame Tipping was the daughter of Colonel Thomas Cheek of Pyrgo, who was Governor of the Tower of London in the reign of Charles II. In 1808 the school was in a poor condition and was pulled down, a new school being built on a new site in North Road in 1818. The new school was poorly built and replaced in 1837 by a National School for 60 children provided by subscription from various local residents and the Church of England. The list of subscribers included Queen Victoria and the Queen Dowager (Adelaide, widow of William IV) who both wished to "promote the restoration of so ancient a charity". The growth of the village meant that the school had to be rebuilt once more in 1891, which is the building that still stands in North Road, incorporating the plaques commemorating the previous buildings of 1724 and 1837.

Cranham's educational benefactor was the Boyd family of Cranham Hall, who founded a school in 1818. Various locations were used before a school for 115 children was built in St Mary's Lane in 1870. The land was given by the new owner of Cranham Hall, Richard Benyon, with the school and school house still standing as a memorial to the work done by the Boyd family. Miss Sarah Boyd ran the new school until 1889, when she moved out of the area. Although the school closed officially in 1950, it was used as temporary accommodation until 1958, when it became the village hall.

The Benyon family also feature in the development of education in North Ockendon. There were various small schools in the parish dating from the 1750s. The first purpose built school was the St Mary's Church of England school, which opened in Church Lane in 1842 on land owned by Richard Benyon of North Ockendon Hall, who owned various other estates, including Cranham Hall. After various enlargements, the school was rebuilt for 80 children in 1902 by James Benyon. The school was in danger of closure in 1947, when there were only 30 pupils but it became an Aided school in 1955 and still stands, although only used as a nursery centre.

Rainham, like the other parishes in the Borough, had various small schools through the centuries which had been set up through bequests. These schools were called 'dame schools', as the education of young children was usually in the hands of mistresses. The parochial school was sited in Upminster Road South, with a new one, that is still standing today, being built in 1872 . Rainham's school board was not formed though until 1893 and a few years later a new school for 300 children was built behind the 1872 building. Unfortunately the new school was destroyed by bombing in the 1939-45 War, with the older building fortunately surviving.

Wennington's children were taught in private houses until 1887, when a school was built on a site next to the churchyard. The school was only built for 60 pupils and became overcrowded by 1906. The county council reorganised the school so that it only took juniors and infants, whereas previously schools of this type catered for all ages up to the leaving age. The school continued as a junior and infants school until 1966, when the building was converted into three dwellings. Although the structure of the school building and school house is still there they have not been included in the list below of old schools as the buildings no longer look like a school now that they have been converted.

The oldest purpose built school building that is still used as a school is the Rainham school built in 1872. The following is a list of the oldest purpose built school buildings that are still standing that still retain their original looks, together with a note of whether they are still used as a London Borough of Havering school. I have not included Hare Hall, the home of the Royal Liberty School, in this list, as this was originally a private residence (see Hare Hall).

| | Built | Still a LA School |
|---|---|---|
| Noak Hill, Church Road | 1848 | No |
| Hornchurch, North Street | 1855 | No |
| Cranham, St Mary's Lane | 1870 | No |
| Rainham, Upminster Road South | 1872 | Yes |
| Romford, Albert Road | 1884 | No |
| Harold Wood, Gubbins Lane | 1886 | No |
| Havering-atte-Bower, North Road | 1891 | Yes |
| Hornchurch, Park Lane | 1893 | No |
| Romford, Mawney Road | 1896 | Yes |
| Hornchurch, Blacksmiths Lane | 1899 | Yes |
| North Ockendon, Church Lane | 1902 | No |

North Ockendon School

## SOUTH HORNCHURCH

In the southern part of Hornchurch we will be covering separately the area to the east, where Suttons Manor stretched from the town centre to what is now the Airfield estate and we have also dealt with Bretons which stands on the west of the Rainham Road. There were though other properties in the South Hornchurch area worthy of mention and these are Whybridge, Mardyke, and the estate known as Maylards Green and Wybridge. Some old maps spell Whybridge and Wybridge the same and historically they were probably connected.

Whybridge farmhouse stood just south of Rainham Road, near Cherry Tree Corner, where Nelson Road and Hubert Road have now been built. The estate can be traced back to the 14th century and the property was also called Rands after John Rand who acquired the land in 1455. Through the centuries the size of the estate changed little, but generally it occupied all the land south of Rainham Road to Dovers Corner and New Road (A13). In 1849 the farm was occupied by the Tyler family and at that time there were 312 acres. The Tylers were followed by Thomas Mashiter, J.P., who was very fond of hunting and racing. Thomas Mashiter donated the funds to covert the old Hornchurch workhouse into almshouses. The property and its grounds must have been very attractive in this mid-19th century period as the property is described as a country seat with gardens, ornamental water and extensive parkland. The house, probably built in the 17th century, was a large farmhouse with some of the rooms being panelled. The main feature of this property seems to have been the grounds which contained a large lake full of fish, walkways lined with statues and an attractive orchard towards Dovers Corner. The estate also had a trotting track where races were held in the 1860s. Farming continued at Whybridge until the 1930s when the farm was sold for residential development.

To the west of Whybridge lay the manor of Mardyke. The land comprising the estate accounted for the residue of the farmland between Whybridge and the Beam River, the boundary between Havering and Dagenham. Once again the manor can be traced back many centuries, with the first reference being in about 1240. Successive manor houses have stood in the area and it does seem that the site favoured was on the edge of the marshland, which in past centuries encroached all the way up to where the A13 road has now been built. This marshland, which stretched the one mile from the Thames to roughly the line of the A13 Road, was not flooded, but just low lying land which was suitable for grazing. A map of 1777 shows the property located roughly where the tower blocks of the Mardyke housing estate are today, at the western end of Frederick Road. It seems that in 1594 Mardyke was an important country seat in this part of the Borough, being the residence of Sir Sebastian Harvey. The last property on the site was Mardyke farm, which did not contain any remains of the former grand residence, which comprised three reception rooms and seven bedrooms together with the usual domestic rooms for the servants. In 1849 the farm comprised 177 acres. The Tyler family were also associated with Mardyke owning the farm from 1734 for over 100 years until well in to the 19th century. The 20th century saw the farmland go for gravel winning with the area around the farmhouse being built on in the 1960s. The second of Hornchurch's windmills, mentioned in the section entitled 'Windmills', would have been on the Mardyke estate and this mill can also trace its history back to 1240.

The other interesting feature in this area is the existence of the old Romford Canal. Just the other side of the River Beam in the parish of Dagenham lies the remains of part of the canal, started in 1875 to connect Romford with the Thames at Dagenham. The line of the canal in this southern part of the Borough was to be close to the river Beam so that little land needed be purchased. The Romford Canal Act, 1875, gave the company the necessary powers and a long section was built in this area by 1880. The canal would have been four and a half miles long if it had been completed but the scheme folded in 1880, with only a small part of the southern section being built. It is surprising that Romford should want to build a canal at this time when railway lines were springing up all over the country.

We now come to the manor of Maylards Green and Wybridge. Although there were two separate farmhouses the properties are linked, as the farms were adjacent and invariably owned by the one landowner. Harrow Lodge Park, Hornchurch, is roughly the site of both farms. Wybridge stood in Upper Rainham Road, where the park meets that road, with the farmland extending into the park south of the brook which is now called the River Ravensbourne, although previously called Bowles Brook. Maylards Green farmhouse stood in the park north of the river near to the present boating lake. The northern part of the park abutting Hornchurch Road was originally part of Suttons manor and later Harrow Lodge was built (see Harrow Lodge). Maylards Green and Wybridge manor was originally part of Hornchurch Priory (see Hornchurch Hall). Both these minor manors are first mentioned in 1237, when land was obtained from the Priory. In 1849 Maylards farm comprised 165 acres and Wybridge farm 276 acres, which together formed an extensive part of the land which is now the southern part of Harrow Lodge Park and the present residential area of Elm Park. Both farmhouses were pulled down in the 1920s. Little is known about either property although the last Wybridge dated from the 16th century, with Maylards being recorded as having 17 hearths in 1670 in connection with the Hearth Tax.

Whybridge

127

## STEWARDS

Although the manor of Stewards was the most central of Romford's historic houses it does not feature to any great extent in the history of the area, as the last house on the site named Stewards was demolished in 1717. The manor though is important in the history of the Borough as regards the area it covered and also in respect of its most notable occupant.

The manor house lay on the east side of South Street, Romford, roughly where the Liberty pedestrian way leads into the main shopping area. The history of the manor can be traced back to at least 1499. At its peak in the 17th century the estate stretched all the way from South Street, called Hornchurch Road at the time, to Squirrels Heath and comprised 374 acres. The house was described as a large 16th century gabled building. In 1618 the grounds were described as parkland, but by 1696 the parkland had been turned into farmland. Following the demolition of the house the records indicated that another house would not be built although the estate land still remained. A new house was built though some time later, but it was called Romford Hall ,which survived right up till 1914. As residential development moved slowly into the 18th and early 19th centuries the old Steward's estate contracted, leaving, by the latter half of the 19th century, only the land that eventually became Western Road, Eastern Road, Junction Road and Victoria Road. The building of the railway to Romford in 1839 had cut the estate in two leaving 255 acres. Little is known about Romford Hall apart from the fact that it was a large red brick building built about 1720, and which lasted for nearly 200 years.

The most notable resident at Stewards was Francis Quarles. His father had purchased the estate in 1588 and Francis was born at Stewards in 1592. Francis was only seven when his father died and fourteen when his mother died. He was educated at Christ's College, Cambridge, and then went to Lincoln's Inn, although he did not take up the legal profession. Francis was a poet and a writer and unfortunately this was his downfall. He sided with Charles I and published a poem supporting the King. With the upsurge of the Parliamentary Party (Cromwell), Francis Quarles upset those heading for power and had his estates and manuscripts seized including all his poems and other writings that were ready for publication. This blow to a man who lived by his pen brought about his early death in 1644 at the age of 52. As a Royalist, Francis Quarles was very popular in the reign of Charles I and, of course, out of favour during the period of the Commonwealth. Even when Charles II came to the throne, some years later, Francis Quarles did not regain his past popularity. Other members of the family resided at Stewards with the estate being kept in the family for nearly 100 years.

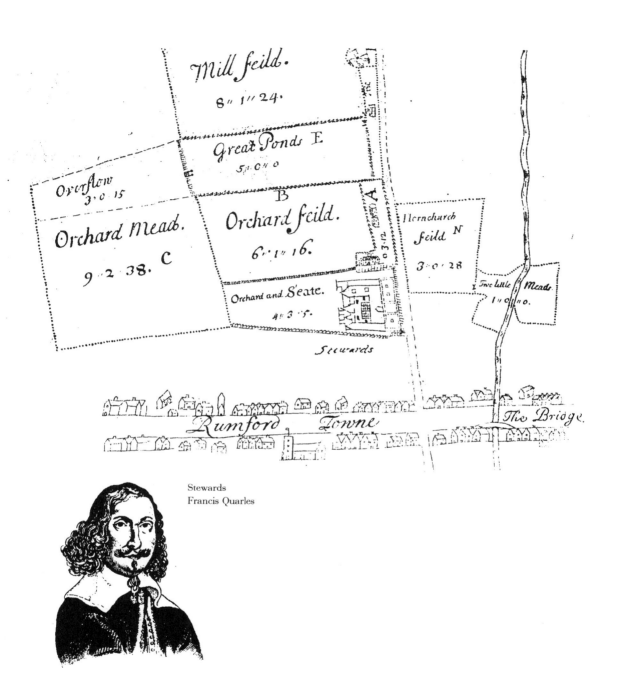

Mill feild.

8 " 1 " 24.

Great Ponds E

5 " 0 " 0

Overflow
3 . 0 . 15

Orchard Mead.

9 . 2 . 38. C

B

Orchard feild.

6 " 1 " 16.

A

Hornchurch
feild N

3 . 0 . 28

Two little Meads

1 " 0 " 0.

Orchard and Seate.

4 " 3 " 5.

Stewards

Rumford Towne

The Bridge

Stewards
Francis Quarles

129

## STREET SCENES - ROMFORD

Although this book is principally about the historic houses and other buildings in the Borough, it would be remiss of me if I did not include some general street scenes of Romford to show what the shopping parades and the market looked like up to a century ago. The old photographs do not feature buildings of any special architectural or historical interest, but are of general interest and highlight the people of the area, their dress and the various modes of transport in the early part of the 20th century. No publication about the Borough would be complete without photographs of the market, which show both sides of Market Place in about 1920. Romford Market was established in 1247 by an order of Henry III addressed to the Sheriff of Essex stating that a market could be held on a Wednesday. In 1250 an order was passed allowing a fair to be held annually during Whit week. Markets were also held on Mondays and Tuesdays in centuries past. but these were discontinued. The Saturday market has been held since the beginning of this century. The market was the property of the Crown and, for example, James I in 1619 leased the market to trustees for the Prince of Wales for a term of 99 years. At the expiry of that lease, subsequent leases were granted to various individuals until finally, the market, along with the Manor of Havering, was bought by Hugh McIntosh of Marshalls in 1828. The market continued to descend with the manor, despite attempts by the Romford Local Board to buy the freehold. The land and the income from the market was eventually purchased by the local authority in 1892 for £7,000 from Mrs McIntosh.

THE MARKET, ROMFORD

ROMFORD, SOUTH STREET & POST OFFICE

South Street, Romford.

Market Place, Romford.

310

## STREET SCENES - COTTAGES

Following on from views of central Romford, which was all hustle and bustle. even a century ago, the other parts of the Borough were sleepy and traffic free with horse-drawn vehicles being the main form of transport. All the houses and cottages featured have long gone and although none were of particular historic interest the scenes give a good idea of the pace of life in the outer areas of the Borough in the early part of this century.

In the north of the Borough the cottages at Collier Row and Havering-atte-Bower were both photographed in about 1910. Collier Row was very much a rural village until 1929 when the first blocks of land were released for residential development. Previously Collier Row had grown very slowly with any new buildings hugging Collier Row Lane up to Chase Cross Road. The only large property in the 19th century was Lawns House, off Lawns Way, built in 1850. The house became a social club, but has now been knocked down for building development. The Collier Row photograph was probably taken in Collier Row Road looking down towards the White Hart public house and the bridge over the River Rom.

The cottages in the photograph of Havering-atte-Bower were just north of the Green in North Road, opposite the Red Lion public house. The view is south towards the Green, which would be on the righthand side.

I have featured two photographs of cottages in the centre of Hornchurch, which were opposite each other. The first shows what is now commonly called Burton's Corner, looking up North Street towards the school on the right which is identified by the bell tower (see Schools). The second view is from the same corner this time looking down the High Street towards Upminster. The cottages and the arch were on the bend opposite where the post office is now.

The Upminster cottages were in Corbets Tey Road, opposite where the park is now, although at the time the photograph was taken the park was a field called the Glebe and belonging to the church. The cottages were called Post Office Cottages, with the post office being housed in the shop at the far end. The last view is of cottages in Cranham Road which is now called St Mary's Lane. The cottages were on the north side of the road with the Masons' Arms being the last property in view.

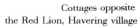
Cottages opposite
the Red Lion, Havering village

134

Cranham Road (now St Mary's Lane) with Masons' Arms in distance

Collier Row

North Street, Hornchurch, looking towards school

Hornchurch High Street at North Street corner

Post Office Cottages, Upminster

## SOUTH HALL MANOR

The old manor house is now called South Hall farm and is situated about three quarters of a mile from the centre of Rainham along the Wennington Road. South Hall manor was mentioned in the Domesday Book and comprised about 480 acres in the 11th century.

Before the Norman Conquest the manor was held by a Saxon freeman called Alfsi, but by the time the Domesday Book was produced in 1086 the manor was held by Bishop Odo of Bayeux, half brother to King William. Frank Lewis, in his history of Rainham, records all the holders of the manor through the centuries, but it is noted that one holder of the manor was summoned before King John for not maintaining the upkeep of the ditches and banks of the marshes. Another was summoned for not keeping clean the River Ingrebourne at Rainham, which caused flooding at Hornchurch and Cranham.

South Hall has never been a large estate compared with others in the Borough area and it is noted that, by 1899, the farm comprised 167 acres, which was sold in two lots in that year. The Gunary family purchased the farm in 1917 and, on his retirement in 1958, Mr H Gunary sold the remaining 105 acres to the Thames Grit and Aggregate Company.

The present farm house dates back to the 16th century, although there have been many later additions, including encasing the front in brick in the 18th century. There are many old internal beams, which have become very hard over the centuries.

# STUBBERS

Stubbers lay just within the parish of North Ockendon and was the second most important estate in that parish after North Ockendon Hall. The house and grounds were south of the Ockendon Road on land now owned by the local authority and used as an Adventure Centre. The first reference to the land which evolved into the Stubbers estate was in 1334, but it was not until 1439 when William and Alice Stubber acquired the property, and various other parcels of land in the area, that the property took on the name we know today. By 1629 the estate had grown to 160 acres, which was not particularly large, with 103 acres being in North Ockendon and the balance in the adjacent parishes of Upminster and Cranham, whose borders abut the North Ockendon Road.

The estate was sold to the Coy family in 1563 and, on the death of Roger Coy, his son, William, inherited the property. From then onwards Stubbers became well known for its collection of plants which came from all over the world. William Coy built four walled gardens to house all his imports which included rhubarb, tomato and yucca which had not been seen before in this country. Fellow botanists also brought trees and plants not found elsewhere to Stubbers to be studied in the grounds. William Coy was also interested in the scientific side of botany and he conducted research into plant breeding and the fermentation of beer, which resulted in today's beer having its bitter flavour by the addition of hops.

The property passed from the Coys through various owners, until Sir Benjamin Wright purchased the estate in 1660. Sir Benjamin also owned the Cranham Hall estate, whose land abutted that of Stubbers, and later in 1673 he bought Great Sunnings farm, Corbets Tey, which was also adjacent to his own land. The Russell family came on to the scene in 1689 and by this time Stubbers had grown to 300 acres. Ownership continued in the same family right up to 1947 when the estate was sold to the Essex Education Committee as a Youth Centre.

The last house was originally Elizabethan and probably built at the time of the Coys, although extensive alterations took place during the time of the Russell family. The photograph shows the north facing front which was built in the late 18th century. In the same period the Russells built a dove cote in 1797, an orangery, stables and kennels. William Russell also kept the Essex Union Hunt pack of hounds at Stubbers in about 1800. The walled gardens made famous by William Coy survived until about 1800 when they were replaced by a crinkle crankle walled garden which still stands today. The house was demolished in 1960, with the site and grounds being transferred to the London Borough of Havering in 1965. A booklet, available from Havering Libraries, has been published, giving in-depth detail of the house and its owners.

Whilst researching Stubbers, I came across some interesting information concerning the road system in the area that also involved another property in North Ockendon parish, which has not been mentioned until now. There is a theory that the reason that many of the parishes in south Essex are long and narrow in a north/south direction is to do with the flow of pilgrims to Canterbury in the Middle Ages who would have crossed the Thames in the Tilbury area or at Rainham Ferry. Many of these 'Green Lanes' have got lost in modern road developments, although the straight road from Pilgrims Hatch through Brentwood and from the Halfway House public house to Orsett and beyond is said to be one of the pilgrim routes. In our own area there was a very straight footpath from The Chase in Cranham, past the church, southwards to Stubbers, which carried right through the estate crossing Dennises Lane and into a farm track which led to Baldwins farm. If you follow these landmarks on a map it is quite possible that this could have been an old pilgrim route to the Thames. Today there is no footpath across Stubbers, because in 1814 John Russell of Stubbers used his influence to have the route diverted with a new road being built to the west of his estate called Stubbers Lane which linked the Ockendon Road to Dennises Lane. It was mentioned above that the original 'Lane' passed Baldwins, which is the oldest farmhouse in North Ockendon parish. Its history can be traced back to the 14th century although the present building is a 16th century timber framed house, which is now empty and in a state of decay.

STUBBERS (North front) UPMINSTER

## GREAT SUNNINGS AND LITTLE SULLENS

These farmhouses stand almost opposite each other in Sunnings Lane, Corbets Tey. Both houses are individually named on the André and Chapman map of Essex of 1777, although the map maker placed Great Sunnings in the Ockendon Road instead of Sunnings Lane. This, incidentally, was one of the few mistakes in this well known map. Little Sullens is spelt `Sunnings' on this map, but in the last century or so it has been spelt `Sullens'.

Both farmhouses can trace their histories back many centuries, with Great Sunnings being the older and historically the more important. Great Sunnings externally has lost much of its historical looks although there is still a jettied west end where the upper floor extends over the lower. Wilson, in his *Sketches of Upminster* in 1856, described Great Sunnings as follows:-

"Upon entering, the form and size of the hinges and bolts of the doors impress us with its antiquity; and in its panelled rooms we discover that it must date at least from the latter part of Elizabeth's reign (1558-1603), and have been the residence of a man of family. The panelling of three of the rooms is as fresh and perfect as when it was put up. It is a good specimen of flat panelling about the end of the 16th century, and the only one in the neighbourhood."

Unfortunately the panelling and an Adam fireplace went to the United States in the late 1940s.

Great Sunnings is mentioned in the reign of Henry VII (1485-1509) in connection with the extermination of wolves in this country. It was decided to levy each estate, according to size, with the number of wolves that they had to exterminate. Great Sunnings had a levy of three per year whereas, by comparison, Stubbers in North Ockendon had a levy of two. This gives some idea of the importance of this house in centuries past.

Some historians say that Little Sullens is an older estate than its neighbour and it is possible that it may date back to the 15th century. The previous house was destroyed by fire in September, 1874, and rebuilt immediately afterwards and so the present house is of no great age compared with Great Sunnings and other farmhouses in the area. Ownership of the farm changed little through the centuries with the estate being willed by Philip Masham in 1692 to the Feltmakers' Company in London and still being in their ownership two hundred years later. The farm was leased out with the income to go to the Feltmakers "to distribute every year at Christmas to 20 decayed hat makers, poor only and not otherwise, be the number more or less, 20 shillings a piece, according as the rents of the estate shall rise or fall; with a reserved annuity of £5 per annum to his kinswoman Katherine Parsons, which upon her death was to augment the fund for the poor hatmakers".

Great Sunnings

Little Sullens

## SUTTONS MANOR

The manor of Suttons was the oldest manor in Hornchurch. Originally the whole of Hornchurch formed part of the royal manor of Havering located at Havering-atte-Bower. Early in the reign of Henry II, he gave two grants of land forming part of his Havering manor to the monastery of St Nicholas and St Bernard of Savoy, which was at the top of the St Bernard Pass between Switzerland and Italy. Apparently an envoy from Henry was given hospitality by the monks and the grant was in appreciation of their assistance. The land, which was granted in about 1159, became known as the Manor of Suttons, the name coming from an early resident of the land. The other grant was in 1163 which was the Church of Havering (St Andrew's) which became the manor of Hornchurch Hall.

In the Middle Ages the Suttons Manor estate occupied all that part of Hornchurch between Abbs Cross Lane in the west, the River Ingrebourne to the east and north/south from High Street, Hornchurch to Dovers Corner on the A13 trunk road. Suttons Lane today starts at Hornchurch Station, but before the railway was built Suttons Lane extended all the way down to the High Street. Previously Suttons Lane was called Lake Street, due to the nearby lake which could well have been on the low lying land adjacent to where Hornchurch station is now.

In 1392 Richard II and the Pope agreed that those lands granted to the monastery could be sold to William of Wykeham, Bishop of Winchester, to endow a college he had built at Oxford, later known as New College. Usually there is a manor house associated with every manor estate, but with Suttons this does not appear to have been the case. As the estate was owned by New College for many centuries this means that there was an absentee landlord and, with no manor house family to house, a manor house did not evolve. There were though a number of large properties on the manor and the largest, which could well have served as a manor house, was Hacton Farm. On the Chapman & André map of 1777 the house appears to be substantial and it is known that a house existed on the site in at least the 16th century. The property is not to be confused with Hactons which is in the parish of Upminster, although Hacton Farm was fairly close, being only a few hundred yards on the Hornchurch side of the river Ingrebourne, roughly where Central Drive is today. The entrance to this large house was off Hacton Lane. At the time of the 1777 map the property was spelt 'Hackton', with the house in Upminster being referred to as Hackton Hill.

The other large properties on the estate were Suttons Gate, Suttons Farm, Elm Farm and Sockets which became known as Albyns Farm. Of all of these only Albyns is still standing, the house dating from the 17th century, although the history of this house goes back much further. The Albyn family is recorded in the 13th century. The present house has undergone alterations through the centuries the latest being a brick front in the 18th century. The house is off South End Road, South Hornchurch, adjacent to the new Hornchurch Country Park.

Suttons Farm dates back to at least 1397, when New College made repairs to the farmhouse. The old farmhouse has long gone with the last building on the site having been erected in Victorian times. In the early 20th century the farm comprised 384 acres. Suttons Farm became the site of the airfield used in the 1914-18 War and once again used as a Battle of Britain airfield in 1939-45. After the first war the land was returned to farm use but in 1924 129 acres were repurchased and turned back into an airfield. Further land was sold to the Air Ministry in 1931. During the 1930s the remainder of the farm was sold for residential development with the Airfield estate using up the last of the available land in the 1970s.

With the coming of the railway that part of Suttons Lane on the Hornchurch town centre side became known as Station Lane and in this section was a property called Suttons Gate. Suttons Gate stood on the opposite side of the road to where Suttons Avenue joins Station Lane where Ravenscourt Grove is today. A house existed on the site from at least the 17th century and there was probably a residence there for a century or two before that. The last house was rebuilt in the late 18th or early 19th century with the drawing being from an old photograph. The house was called Suttons Gate as there was originally a gate across Suttons Lane (Station Road) on the north side of the house to stop villagers from Hornchurch approaching the property and having access to the Suttons manor estate where the road in past centuries was across private land. It appears that the gate was removed in about 1840, although with the sparseness of population in Hornchurch at that time there would have been little need for anyone to go farther up Suttons Lane as the road only led to Suttons Farm. It would not have been until 1885 when the railway came to Hornchurch and the station was built that there would have been any need to proceed further up Suttons Lane past Suttons Gate. This Georgian property was finally demolished in 1936 to make way for residential development.

Although most of the land that comprised the original Suttons manor estate had been sold prior to the 1939-45 War, residential development did not recommence until after the War and by this time all that was left of the old manor was the ex-RAF airfield. This was sold in lots from 1963 when the Airfield residential estate was built leaving only a small area which has now been turned into Hornchurch Country Park.

## WENNINGTON HALL

Wennington Hall can trace its history back to the Domesday Book and was probably in existence in the 10th century, as the hamlet of Wennington, then called Winintuna, was mentioned as early as 969. In the early 11th century the manor was held by Edward the Confessor and after the Conquest it was held by Westminster Abbey at the time the Domesday Book was compiled in 1086. Many notable figures held Wennington Hall in the Middle Ages although it is unlikely that many actually lived at Wennington as noblemen in those times invariably held many manors in the same county. In the latter part of the 14th century the manor was held by Sir John Gildesburgh who was Speaker in the parliaments of Richard II. About the same time Henry Yevelle, who was responsible for the building of the nave of Westminster Abbey and also worked on Canterbury cathedral, held Wennington.

The present Wennington Hall stands at the end of Wennington Road, where it meets New Road the A13. The Hall was rebuilt in 1854 and it stands on the site of previous manor houses, although there have been many alterations since. Unfortunately the property no longer has that manor house look about it being transformed into a modern 20th century building.

## TYLER'S HALL

Tylers Hall stands on the north east corner of Upminster Common and is approached from a drive off Nag's Head Lane. In the early part of the 19th century common land comprised three of the segments of the cross roads at Hall Lane/Nag's Head Lane and Shepherd's Hill. The area on which Tyler's Hall stands was originally called Tyler's Common with that on the western side of Nag's Head Lane and Hall Lane called Upminster Common or Gaynes Common as it was originally part of the Gaynes manor estate. The land on which Tyler's Hall stands was once part of Upminster Hall manor.

The derivation of the name Tyler's Hall is from Tylehurst or Tigelhurst, which is a combination of two Saxon words signifying a wood and earth suitable for making bricks and tiles. The land still contains brick earth, as does all the land from the common back to Bird Lane, Upminster, where the Upminster brickfields were located.

The common land that was Gaynes Common was enclosed in the mid-19th century, leaving what is now Upminster Common and Tyler's Hall, which itself comprised 198 acres in the 1880s. We are not sure of the exact age of the house, but it was certainly there in 1777, when it appeared on the Chapman and André map as one of the principal properties in Upminster. It is a typical Essex weatherboarded house and it seems that at the time of the above map part of the house was the 'farm end' and part the 'family apartment'. The probable date of construction was the early 18th century and it is quite likely that there was a farm on the site previously.

The second photograph is that of the pond just south of the house and was taken at least 60 years ago. The pond is still there but much overgrown, but this could be near the site of the historic mineral spring, which was 150 yards south of the farmhouse. The spring was first noticed by Dr Dereham (1657-1735), rector of St Laurence, Upminster. The soil on the common is sand and clay and usually impervious to water. Springs rarely force there way through, but when they do the water is impregnated with mineral salts which have been drawn out of the clay. The spring near Tyler's Hall has been mentioned by various past historians, but it does not seem that the waters ever attained great repute. One historian recommended  the water for the treatment of "agues and dropsies being the common diseases of the county".

As Tyler's Hall was for many centuries part of the Upminster Hall estate the occupiers were tenants and it is noted that Andrew Branfill of Upminster Hall let the farmhouse to his son-in-law Captain John Redman and his daughter Mary in the 1770s. The farm was later sold out of the manor estate.

Tylers Hall                                                                    Upminster Hall

# UPMINSTER HALL

Upminster Hall stands off Hall Lane, Upminster, and is now the clubhouse for the Upminster Golf Club. It was one of seventeen manors, mostly in Essex, given to Waltham Abbey in the 11th century. Edward the Confessor had originally given the Abbey and its estates to Earl Harold Godwinson, who later became King Harold II, and, although he was defeated at Hastings, the new Norman régime upheld the charter granted in 1062, which established the abbey and its lands.

Little seems to have disturbed the monks at Upminster for the next few hundred years and it is probable that their estate at Upminster was a retreat or hunting lodge, according to the historian Morant, to which they would invite their influential guests. At the time of the Domesday Book the manor covered about 1,500 acres which was half the area of Upminster and roughly accounted for all the land from the centre of Upminster to Upminster Common at Nag's Head Lane.

The Hall had its own chapel, with the font now residing in St Laurence church, Upminster. The chapel was taken down by a subsequent owner, but there are stories of vaults below the chapel which may still exist. The oldest part of the present building is dated at 1450, with the staircase and gallery of the time of Charles I (1625-49). The house was originally moated with only a pond at the rear of the house reminding us of this feature. The adjacent barn (the Tithe Barn) is also dated at about 1450. With the Dissolution of the Monasteries the Waltham Abbey estates were broken up and in 1540 Upminster Hall manor was granted to Thomas Cromwell, the Lord Privy Seal, the right hand man of Henry VIII. Cromwell lost his head in 1543 and once again the manor reverted to the King.

Upminster Hall was purchased from the Crown by Ralph Latham, who had bought Gaynes manor in the same year (see Gaynes manor). This meant that Latham now owned the two largest estates in Upminster and virtually the whole of the village. The Latham family held the manor for 99 years and after passing through a number of hands the Branfil family acquired the estate in 1685. Once again a long family association with the property was started, which lasted until 1906, when much was sold for residential development. The lordship was eventually acquired by Essex County Council in 1938, with the house and six and a half acres being acquired in 1935 by the Upminster Golf Club, who also bought the land on the west side of Hall Lane to complete the golf course.

It is interesting to note that during the 900 years from when Waltham Abbey acquired Upminster Hall manor the property was only held by three owners for nearly 850 years.

# WINDMILLS

We are fortunate in having a very good example of a windmill still standing within the Borough and most travellers to Upminster, by road or train, cannot fail to see the mill that proudly stands at the top of Upminster Hill. Windmills date back to the 12th century as before that there were only water mills. There are basically two types of windmill - post mills and smock mills. The earlier variety is the post mill, which had a box shaped body which carried the sails and the machinery. The body and sails were mounted on a large upright oaken post with the whole structure being turned by manpower so that the sails faced the wind. Much effort was needed to turn the body of a post mill and consequently their size was limited. By the 14th century a better type of windmill was invented, originally known as a tower mill, consisting of a stone or brick tower body on top of which was a cap and the sails with only the cap and sails being turned into the wind. Where there was an absence of stone or brick the tower was built of wood which was generally an eight sided tapering body looking like a farm labourer's smock. Upminster's is a smock mill: a good example of a post mill is at Ingatestone.

There are various references to windmills in the records over the centuries, but I will just concentrate on those that can be traced with some certainty during recent centuries. The map shows the rough position of eleven windmills of which ten were in operation at the same time. The windmill in South Hornchurch had been demolished before the one on Upminster Hill had been built in 1802/3. The following chart sets out the eleven mills, their type and location, and roughly when they ceased operation.

## ROMFORD

Pratt Collier's Mill, south of London Road near St Andrew's Road: Post mill - ceased c.1860

Edward Collier's Mill, south of Main Road near Pettits Lane: Post mill - ceased c.1860

Rising Sun Mill, behind the Rising Sun public house in Victoria Road: Post mill - ceased c.1876

Collier Row Mill, west of Lawns Way, off Chase Cross Road: Post mill - ceased c. 1860s

Mark's Gate Mill, Whalebone Lane North: Smock mill - ceased c. 1890

## HORNCHURCH

Mitchell or Howard's Mill, 300 yards to rear of St Andrew's Church: Post mill - ceased 1912

Mardyke Mill, south of Rainham Road and east of Beam River: Post mill - ceased 1700s

Bush Elms Mill, north of Hornchurch Road, south of Hylands Park: Post mill - ceased 1864

## UPMINSTER

Upminster Mill, St Mary's Lane on hill on road from Hornchurch to Upminster: Smock mill - ceased 1934

Upminster Common Mill, off Ivy Lodge Lane, Shepherd's Hill: Post mill - ceased c.1880

## NORTH OCKENDON

North Ockendon Mill, Fen Lane leading to Bulphan, half a mile from junction with South Ockendon Road: Post mill - ceased 1840

Of the eleven mills, nine were post mills and two were smock. The two smock mills were the last two built at Upminster and Mark's Gate, in 1802 and 1818 respectively,

Upminster Windmill

Drake's Windmill, Marks Gate

Hornchurch Windmill

149

reflecting the change in building design in the 19th century.

The Collier family ran two Romford windmills in the 19th century: this family name can be found in parish records from the early 1680s. There are not always the records available to pinpoint the date that windmills were built and one has to rely on maps of the period or trade directories which listed all the businesses in an area and who ran them. Running a business does not mean that the person owns the site. The first indication of the windmill near St Andrew's Road, came from a map of 1728, which, coincidentally, was the first indication of the other Collier mill to the south of Main Road, near Pettits Lane, mentioned in a will of 1728. It does seem, though, the mill on the eastern side of the town had a history going back farther than 1728, although earlier references to the windmill in this part of Romford placed it on the north of Main Road. The photograph of the watercolour of the Rising Sun mill puts the mill behind the old Rising Sun public house, wedged between the railway line and Victoria Road. This mill also has a long history and appeared on a map of Havering dated 1618. When the railway came to Romford in 1840 the high embankment built to carry the line over South Street cut off the wind to the mill and effectively brought to an end its usefulness. Fortunately industrialisation had brought about the invention of the steam mill, which was built alongside the old windmill. The windmill lasted in its unused state until it was pulled down about 1880.

Collier Row windmill was built about 1810 as a post mill, which is interesting as designs were now changing to the smock mill, like the new one built at Upminster a few years earlier. The location was what is now Lawns Park, off Lawns Way. William Blakeley, who married into the Collier family, was the owner and occupier in 1846 and he is said to have built Lawn House, which has recently been pulled down for building development. The windmill ceased operations in about 1860 and had gone by 1870. All the four Romford windmills featured so far had stopped operating by the 1860/70s and the main reason would appear to be the steam mill built in Victoria Road, which put an end to the need for wind power. The fifth Romford windmill was at Mark's Gate, off Whalebone Lane North, half a mile north of the junction with Eastern Avenue. The mill was on the eastern side of the road, almost on the border with Dagenham. This mill seems to have been operational from 1818 to about 1890.

The most well known of Hornchurch's three windmills was that behind St Andrew's in an area known locally as The Dell. This piece of land between the church and the mill had been scooped out for gravel reclamation some centuries before and in Victorian times the resulting undulating area was a favourite beauty spot for local residents and also the venue for wrestling and prize fighting. The windmill and its adjacent cottage (still standing) was at the southern end of The Dell and its history can be traced back to 1262, although the last mill on the site was built shortly before 1666 and continued to operate until 1912. A steam mill had been built adjacent to the mill in the 1860s when, like the Romford mills, there was no longer any need for wind power. The mill burnt down in 1921.

Like the windmill at The Dell, the Mardyke mill could also trace its history back to the 13th century. A windmill is recorded in 1240 and this was superseded by another, which

Upminster Common Windmill

The Rising Sun and windmill

was in existence in 1564. This post mill lasted until about 1750, but it was not rebuilt again, although references to Mill Field still existed until recent times for an area south of Rainham Road, fairly close to Newtons Corner.

Hornchurch's third windmill stood on the old Bush Elms Farm, roughly south of Hylands Park, where Hillcrest Road is today. The age of the mill is not known, but it appears to have been a very small mill only used by the farm and not for milling outside trade. It was put up for sale in 1855 and does not appear on a map dated 1864.

Upminster's well known smock mill was built in 1802/3. James Nokes, who was the tenant of Hunts Farm, acquired from Bridge House Farm all the land from the River Ingrebourne to Hall Lane (not then Station Road) on the north side of St Mary's Lane. The mill, mill-house and cottages were built on the brow of the hill and a bakery and cottages (which existed until 1953) in Station Road. It seems that a steam engine was installed by 1811 to supplement the wind power, which was very early in the development of these machines. Many articles and books have been written recording the history and trials and tribulations of the windmill during its life and consequently I will not go into detail in this work. Suffice to say the windmill is still with us and, now in the care of the local authority, its future is assured.

The photograph of the post mill at Upminster Common is from an engraving by B A Branfil of Upminster Hall in September, 1880. Upminster's commons were a lot larger a century ago and, in fact, common land extended on both sides of Shepherd's Hill, abutting Nag's Head Lane and Hall Lane. What we have left now is Tyler's Common on the east of Nag's Head Lane, but the windmill was on Upminster or Gaynes Common, north of Shepherd's Hill, opposite the entrance to Pages Farm. We have no exact date for its construction, but it was probably in existence in 1665. It was pulled down in 1882.

North Ockendon's windmill was not centrally located but half a mile down Fen Lane towards Bulphan. The first reference was in 1610 when a survey of the manor of North Ockendon (Hall) showed that a cottage and windmill were in the occupation of John Cramphorn, a name still associated with Essex agriculture. There is an interesting letter from the miller in 1825 protesting to the owner of adjacent land. Apparently the trees in a field adjoining the mill had grown so high and thick that they took the wind from the sails when it was blowing in a west or south-westerly direction. The miller went on to say that the wind blows in this direction for the majority of the summer and consequently he required the trees to be thinned. We do not know the outcome of the letter, but the mill continued to function for a few more years before being pulled down about 1840.

## WORKHOUSES, ALMSHOUSES AND HOSPITALS

In the above categories there are only three historic buildings still remaining. Upminster's Poor House or Workhouse is now a row of cottages called Ingrebourne Cottages, at the foot of Upminster Hill opposite Bridge Avenue. The former Romford Union Workhouse is now part of Oldchurch Hospital and the Victoria Cottage Hospital in Pettits Lane, Romford is still there, but no longer used as a hospital, although still used for out-patient departments.

The Poor House in a parish was invariably administered by the Vestry, the parish's governing body and the predecessor of the Parish Council. Prior to the Local Government Act of 1894, which authorised every parish to form a parish council, the running of a parish was in the hands of principal local residents who usually met in the church vestry - which is how this body got its name.

Almshouses were usually founded by a local wealthy resident who bequeathed land and money to enable the almshouse to be built with funds to be invested with the income to be used for the upkeep of the house and its residents. Poor Houses were also set up by wealthy residents, but in their case the upkeep was financed out of the local rates. Consequently the poor of a parish were always a problem for the Vestry and if one reads local Vestry minutes (Essex Record Office) it is clear that much time and money was spent discussing the needs of the poor of the parish. In earlier times the poor were lodged with other villagers for a fee but soon it became more economical, both for financial and administrative reasons, to acquire a large property in which the poor could be housed with a poorhousemaster appointed on a salary to run the establishment.

The Vestry at Havering-atte-Bower passed a resolution in 1677 that the overseer for the poor should purchase pewter badges with the seal of the Liberty of Havering engraved thereon to be worn by all persons of the parish that were in receipt of poor relief. This was a common practise in many parishes and it seems that the parish did not ever have its own workhouse which is understandable as the village was so small. The Vestry minutes record that they were threatening to withdraw relief to a certain villager if she did not wear her badge which was to be stitched to her clothing.

Most of the other parishes which make up the Borough had their own workhouses, with Rainham's poor going to Wennington, where there was established a joint workhouse with Aveley and West Thurrock in 1808. North Ockendon's poor in 1786 totalled 120 of which 85 were either in the workhouse or in lodgings, with 35 being lodged in South Ockendon. When one sees that North Ockendon's population in 1801 was only 243 it seems that about half were being supported by the parish. This must have made the rates rather high for the other half. Upminster's poor house was built in 1750 and extended in 1786. In 1803 there were 37 inmates which was the peak figure although in that year North Ockendon's number was down to 21. It appears that many of North Ockendon's poor had been permanently transferred to either the poor house at Great Warley or South Ockendon. Cranham's Vestry petitioned the lord of the manor (Cranham Hall) for a grant of land on which to build a poor house. A piece of land was sold for this purpose to the Vestry for £20 the site being roughly where the Jobbers' Rest is today in St Mary's Lane.

Upminster workhouse,
Upminster Bridge

Romford Union

Roger Reede's Almshouses,
Romford

Wennington poor house was not demolished until 1966 and it is interesting to note that in Cranham's case the income from the sale of the poor house did not go back to the parish, which had bought the land originally, but the proceeds went to the Romford Union.

Hornchurch seems to have had a number of wealthy residents, who established charities for the poor. Many just gave funds to be invested for the benefit of the poor, but John Pennant in his will of 1598 gave four cottages at the corner of High Street and Billet Lane (now Sainsburys) in trust as free dwellings for Hornchurch's poor. In 1721 the site was converted into the parish workhouse and remained as such until the formation of the Romford Union in 1834 when the property was converted back into almshouses. There were also almshouses on the other side of the High Street known as Appleton's Almshouses towards North Street with various buildings exiting there until demolition in 1967.

Romford, as the largest parish in the Borough, had a large poor population with many houses being either owned or leased by the parish in the 18th century. The problem was solved in 1786 with the passing of the Romford Workhouse Act which, like the national Act of 1834, passed the responsibility of Romford's poor from the Vestry to a new corporate body with directors and guardians. Land was purchased in North Street, Romford (then called Collier Row Lane) for the building of a workhouse. The site was on the west side on North Street on land bought from the Roger Reede Trust where his almshouses were adjacent. The workhouse became obsolete in 1834 and was pulled down in 1840 when the inmates were transferred to the Romford Union (now part of Oldchurch Hospital).

Parish Workhouses were abolished in 1834 with the passing of the Poor Law Amendment Act which grouped parishes into Unions who then became responsible for all the poor in its parishes. The Romford Union comprised all the parishes that now fall within the Borough.The Romford Union Workhouse was built in 1838 in Oldchurch Road, Romford and in 1891 the foundation stone was laid for an infirmary, which was adjacent, which comprised a wing for men and one for women with a small office block linking the two. Records for 1896 show that there were 391 inmates in the workhouse and a further 130 patients in the infirmary. The workhouse was a square structure with buildings on all four sides and with a cruciform block in the centre. The workhouse buildings are still almost complete today and used as hospital offices and specialist departments. One of the two infirmary wards is also still standing (two storeys) and used as hospital wards today. Both the workhouse blocks and the remaining one wing of the infirmary are worth a visit (fronting Oldchurch Road) to imagine how the poor and the infirm lived a century ago.

The Roger Reede almshouses were founded in 1482 and in his will of 1483 he gave further land to maintain the property. The almshouses were rebuilt in 1784 housing only about 12 persons. Through the years the land owned by the charity, with the exception of a field north of the market, was sold off and when in 1959 the almshouses in North Street were sold the proceeds were used to build 38 new almshouses on the one piece of land the charity still retained which was originally called Redyn Field. These almshouses are to be found in Church Lane, off St Edwards Way.

The first hospital in the Borough was the Victoria Cottage Hospital, Pettits Lane,

Romford. The land was donated by William Mashiter, who lived in Main Road in a house where the Police Station and Court are now. The hospital opened in 1888. There were various extensions to this small hospital in 1924 and 1939, but at its peak it still only boasted 100 beds. All the buildings are still standing and used by Havering Hospitals for outpatient purposes. We saw earlier that the Romford Union Workhouse had opened an infirmary only a few years after the Cottage Hospital had been established which possibly took some of the pressure off the Pettits Lane hospital for those patients who could not afford to pay hospital fees. The Cottage Hospital lasted well into the 20th century, but although still in the possession of the local health authority, it is now used for other purposes. Oldchurch Hospital was built in 1924 and on the dissolution of the poor-law union in 1930 the institution and the infirmary were incorporated into the hospital with the whole being taken over by Essex County Council. During the 1930s there were still inmates in the workhouse section, but by 1938 they had all been transferred to Sutton's Institution in Hornchurch.

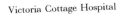

Victoria Cottage Hospital

# LISTED BUILDINGS

You may be surprised to known that there are about 125 buildings or structures within the London Borough of Havering that have 'Listed' status. I use the word 'structure' to include things like the entrance gates and piers at Upminster Court or the walls surrounding Cranham Hall. Many of the listed buildings have been featured in previous pages when information is known about the building and its inhabitants to justify a page or two to themselves. There follows a full list of all the listed buildings as at the date of publication, which in addition to being a record for future reference, gives readers some idea of how well off the Borough is for old buildings in an age were redevelopment is taking place all the time. We are fortunate that being one of the outer London Boroughs our boundary abuts the countryside and many of the listed buildings, especially cottages, are in the Green Belt area, where development is protected.

## ANCIENT MONUMENTS

Upminster Hall barn - known as Tithe Barn
The moated site at Dagnam Park, Harold Hill
Roman road across Romford golf course

## LISTED BUILDINGS

### GRADE 1

St Andrew's Parish Church, Hornchurch
St Helen & St Giles Parish Church, Rainham
St Laurence Parish Church, Upminster
St Mary Magdalene Parish Church, North Ockendon
The Bower House, Orange Tree Hill, and the Stable Block

High House, Corbets Tey

### GRADE 2*

St Edward the Confessor Parish Church, Romford
Royal Liberty School (part formerly Hare Hall)
Bretons, Rainham Road
Bretons, Wrought iron screen and gates with piers
Upminster Windmill
Upminster Hall, Hall Lane
High House Farmhouse, Corbets Tey
Great Tomkyns, Tomkyns Lane, and Barn
The Round House, Broxhill Road
Rainham Hall, The Broadway

Rainham Hall, Forecourt railings, gates and piers
Rainham Hall, Stable Block
The Lodge, Rainham Hall
St Mary & St Peter Parish Church, Wennington

The Old Anchor, Corbets Tey

## GRADE 2

*Collier Row*
Maypole Cottage, Collier Row Road

*Corbets Tey*
The Old Cottage
The Old Anchor
Harwood Hall
Nos 1 - 8 Harwood Hall Lane
Great Sunnings
Little Sullens
Bramble farmhouse

*Cranham*
Cranham Hall
Cranham Hall garden walls
All Saints Parish Church
Pike Lane - Barn & stable block to the north of Broadfields farm

Rose Cottage, Havering-atte-Bower

*Gidea Park*
The Ship public house
Black's Bridge, (Raphael's Park), Main Road
Heath Drive - section of boundary wall of former Gidea Hall
Nos 36 & 38 Reed Pond Walk
Nos 16 & 27 Meadway
Nos 198 & 200 Main Road
Nos 43 & 64 Heath Drive

*Havering-atte-Bower*
The Thatch Cottage, Broxhill Road
Stocks & Whipping Post, Village Green
St John the Evangelist Parish Church
The Green, 1-5 North Side
Rose Cottage, North Road
Ivy Holt, North Road

158

Blue Boar Hall, Orange Tree Hill
Bower Farm Cottage, Orange Tree Hill

## Hornchurch

Langtons, Billet Lane, Gazebo, Orangery and Stable Block
Fairkytes, Billet Lane
King's Head public house, High Street
Nos 195 & 197 High Street
Wykeham Cottage, 218 High Street
Mill Cottage, Mill Fields, High Street
St Leonard's Childrens Home - Hall
Bretons - Two brick barns and garden wall
Albyn's Farm house, South End Road and Barn
Dury Falls, Upminster Road
Lilliputs, Wingletye Lane
Essex Water Company sub station, Dagenham Road
Well Tower (Nelmes Manor), Tower Lodge, Sylvan Avenue

Blue Boar Hall, Havering-atte-Bower

## Noak Hill/Harold Hill

St Thomas Parish Church, Church Road
Morris Dancer public house, Melksham Close
Orchard Cottage, Noak Hill Road
Rose Cottage, Noak Hill Road
Holly Tree Cottage, Noak Hill Road
Meadow Cottages, Noak Hill Road
Old Keeper's Cottage, Noak Hill Road
Thatched Cottage, Noak Hill Road
Angel Cottage, Wrightsbridge Road - now part of Brentwood Borough

Redbury (or Redberry), Rainham

## North Ockendon

The Old Bakehouse, 'Kilbro', Ockendon Road
The Forge, Ockendon Road
Russell Cottage, Ockendon Road
The Rectory, Church Lane
North Ockendon Hall garden walls, Church Lane
Stubbers garden walls, Ockendon Road

## Rainham and Wennington

Berwick Manor Public House, Berwick Pond Road
No 29 The Broadway - 'Redbury'
The Vicarage, The Broadway

Gerpins farmhouse garden wall
Nos 2-8 (even) Upminster Road South
South Hall Farm, Wennington Road
The Willows, New Road, Wennington

*Romford*
Golden Lion public house, High Street
Crown Farm, London Road, and the Granary
Salem Chapel, London Road
Upper Bedfords Farm, Lower Bedfords Road
The Lamb public house, Market Place
Church House, Market Place
Vine Cottage, 215, 215A & 217 North Street
Nos 96-102 (even), North Street
St Andrews Parish Church, St Andrews Road
Warren Farm Barn, Whalebone Lane North
World War II anti-aircraft site, Whalebone Lane North
Various marker stones and coal duty boundary posts

96-102 North Street, Romford

*Upminster*
Clockhouse, St Mary's Lane
Ingrebourne Cottages, St Mary's Lane
Berry/Bury Farm, St Mary's Lane
Nos 265/267 St Mary's Lane
Tylers Hall, Upminster Common
Apse Tree Cottages, Hall Lane
Upminster Court, Hall Lane, Stable Block and entrance gates
The Rectory, St Mary's Lane
No 201 Corbets Tey Road
Tadlows, 251 Corbets Tey Road
Parklands Park, The Bridge, Corbets Tey Road
Pages Farm, Shepherd's Hill
Old Chapel, St Mary's Lane

*Great Warley*
Frank's Farm, St Mary's Lane
Hole Farm, Hole Farm Lane      } Due to boundary changes
Brick House, Warley Street      } now part of Brentwood Borough
Hulmers, Warley Street      }

Pages Farm, Shepherds Hill

The Ancient Monuments are mentioned in a later section and all the Grade 1 and Grade

160

The Old Cottage, Corbets Tey

Maypole Cottage, Collier Row

Bearblock Cottages, Corbets Tey

The Thatched Cottage,
Broxhill Road

Bramble Farm,
Corbets Tey

Cottages in Main Road
(Hare Street)

162

The Ancient Monuments are mentioned in a later section and all the Grade 1 and Grade 2 (star) Listed Buildings are referred to earlier in this work, with the exception of High House Farmhouse, Corbets Tey, which has only recently had its grading improved from Grade 2 to Grade 2 star. This leaves the ordinary Grade 2 buildings without a star. Many have been featured earlier in this work with the residue having been photographed and included in the following pages with a few snippets of information about some of the properties.

The only property of note at Collier Row is Maypole Cottage, a timber framed house built in the late 17th or early 18th century. By its size it can hardly be called a cottage and when photographed it was in course of renovation.

Moving to Corbets Tey there are five Listed properties not featured elsewhere. Four are all clustered around Corbets Tey Village with The Old Cottage and The Old Anchor having both been public houses in the past. The Anchor was an inn from the 17th century, closing in 1896 about the time the Huntsman and Hounds was rebuilt. Almost opposite is The Old Cottage which was an inn called the Royal George in 1789, subsequently becoming The George. In a directory of 1835 the name had changed to the George and Dragon. As a public house it finally closed its doors in 1901. The house is thought to be 400 years old. The living quarters for the old forge next door have now been incorporated into the property which contains oak beams said to have come from galleons at Grays. This leaves the cottages in Harwood Hall Lane and Bramble Farmhouse which, although Listed, have no other features of note. Mention must be made though of High House Farmhouse at the top of Corbets Tey hill which has the prestigious Grade 2 star rating. For many years this old farmhouse was just grade 2, but I presume a survey has been carried out which has highlighted its internal features. I note from the Department of the Environment schedule that this property is dated about 1700, although the wings are much earlier. The star grading has been achieved due to the internal decorations of the property which are said to be virtually completely original. Mention is made of the full panelling to both ground and first floors with rich cornices throughout. Moulded chimney pieces of the period survive in many rooms with corner fireplaces in the front rooms. The staircase is original which has cut strings and pairs of barleysugar twist balusters to each tread. The front room on the ground floor has a fine example of Rococo plasterwork ceiling and the schedule ends up with the observation that the internal of the property is "a remarkable survival of fine quality".

All Cranham's Listed buildings have been covered elsewhere, as have Gidea Park's with the exception of 198-200 Main Road, now part of the The Archers' Restaurant. These former cottages are all that remains of the hamlet of Hare Street. Moving to Havering-atte-Bower the Thatch Cottage in Broxhill Road is a good example of an early 19th century thatched house being only one of two Listed thatched houses in the Borough. Rose Cottage is possibly the oldest cottage in this area with a construction date of 1750 or earlier. This timber framed weatherboarded cottage served as the village store in the 1920s taking on the Post Office in about 1928 and remaining as such until the shop closed in

Ivy Holt, Havering

Bower Farm Cottage, Havering

The Green. Havering-atte-Bower

195-197 High Street, Hornchurch

Wykeham Cottage, 218 High Street, Hornchurch

1970. Blue Boar Hall has an interesting story to tell for as the name suggests it was a public house in at least 1710 and possibly earlier although it was no longer licensed in 1773. There is a story that a Havering archer claimed to have shot a blue boar in the area and when Elizabeth I heard about this when she was staying at Havering Palace she sent for him to ask if it was true. The archer said that the boar turned blue with fear when he saw the arrow. He went on to say, "Blue I saw him as plain as I see the cup of good Essex ale your grace hath ordered your servant to give me at my outgoing". It is said that the Queen was impressed by his humour and frequently invited the archer to the palace.

Next we come to Hornchurch, with the only Listed buildings not mentioned elsewhere being cottages in the High Street, which is really all that is left of old Hornchurch. The properties next door to the King's Head public house, numbered 195 and 197 High Street, are of the 17th century with number 218 High Street, near the church - originally two cottages - being 18th century.

Noak Hill Road and Wrightsbridge Road are on the Borough's northern boundary and truly rural roads, albeit very close to the Harold Hill estate. These two roads contain seven listed cottages with six being 17th and 18th century and Angel Cottage dating back to the 15th century. Angel Cottage is the oldest surviving property in the Borough and its history is linked with Wrightsbridge, a property only 150 yards to the north and right on the South Weald parish border. Wrightsbridge is not a listed building, although its history dates back to the 14th century, as the present house was remodelled in 1926, although the structure has its origins in the 18th century. There is, on the front of the house, a sundial dated 1663, which is impressive and adds character to this attractive property. There is a theory that the original house on the Wrightsbridge estate eventually became Angel cottages when a new property was built farther north. Angel cottage was previously called Little Wrightsbridge and is a timber framed house of the late 14th or early 15th century. In the early 18th century the property became detached from Wrightsbridge, becoming a public house by 1744 and later being converted into two cottages. The two cottages now form one house.

The small parish of North Ockendon has three listed houses not mentioned elsewhere of which two were connected with local businesses. All three are in Ockendon Road near to the junction with Fen Lane. The Forge is the oldest and the village blacksmith had his premises in the workshop next door. The photograph is taken from the back garden of the house with the old blacksmith's smithy still standing and fronting the main road. The house is listed as being of the 17th century but there is evidence of internal woodwork joinery which could date part of the structure as 15th century. The Old Bakehouse is 17th century and was the local bakery and baker's shop. The shop window and shop door have gone and the property is now a private house. Russell Cottage is a good example of a 19th century house whose exterior has remained unchanged.

Rainham and Wennington - Redbury has been mentioned previously under Rainham Village, but I am including an up-to-date photograph of this house which has virtually remained unchanged externally since it was built in the 18th century. The row of cottages

Meadow Cottages, Noak Hill

Thatched Cottage, Noak Hill Road

Holly Tree Cottage, Noak Hill

Old Keeper's Cottage, Noak Hill

Rose Cottage, Noak Hill

Orchard Cottages, Noak Hill

Angel Cottage, Noak Hill

Russell Cottage, North Ockendon

The Forge, North Ockendon

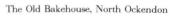

The Old Bakehouse, North Ockendon

2-8 Upminster Road South, Rainham

at 2-8 (even) Upminster Road South have lost their Essex original weatherboarding as shown in the 1950s photograph and these four cottages were originally residential. One still remains so but the other three have been shops for many years. The Willows at Wennington is a 17th century house, but much altered in recent years.

Romford comes next and the Listed buildings not so far mentioned are Vine House at 215/217 North Street, which is now a row of shops, and 96-102 North Street, which sadly are also shops and not at all looking like late 17th century cottages. Vine House is at the northern end of North Street and bears the date 1799. Out of town towards Chadwell Heath on the London Road is Crown Farm, which lies up a long track half way between the London Road and the Eastern Avenue. Crown Farm was previously called Pigtails and is a late 16th or early 17th century house with some later additions. This farm also has an old granary which has achieved Listed status.

Upminster has a handful of sundry listed houses, the oldest being Pages Farm, just within the parish boundary on Shepherd's Hill. The farmhouse is dated 1663 being the date on a corbel supporting an oak beam in one of the ground floor rooms. One of the owners of the farm at the end of the 18th century was the Rector of St Laurence, Upminster, who leased out this small farm to Thomas Wadsworth. The Rector had the right to collect tithes from his parishioners to carry on the work of the church. Historically the tithe was one tenth of the parishioners income or one tenth of his crop or stock. Gradually tithes were converted from kind to cash but with rising inflation at the end of the 18th century these fixed cash sums meant that the Rector's income in real terms was reducing. Consequently the Rector, John Rose Holden, notified certain parishioners, including Thomas Wadswoth, that he was reverting from cash to kind which caused a furore in the village. Within the year the Rector resigned and was succeeded by his son. Upminster Court calls for comment for, although it was only built in 1905/6, it was designed by Sir Charles Reilly, the architect, who lived at High House, Upminster. This large house was built for A E Williams of Samuel Williams & Sons, Ltd. of Dagenham Dock. The house with 22 acres was bought in 1946 by Essex County Council as educational offices and in 1970 Havering Council took it over for the same use. The property is now a Council training centre. The large stable block together with the entrance gates and piers are all listed structures.

The final area in this schedule of listed buildings is Great Warley. Most of the old parish of Great Warley falls within the Brentwood area, but part is within the Borough of Havering. We have already mentioned Franks Farm within the main body of this work and this leaves Hole Farm, Hulmers and Brick House. Hole Farm is approached from Hole Farm Lane, which starts in Brentwood Borough at the Thatchers public house crossroads. The farmhouse is a 16/17th century timber framed building with various internal alterations, although the timber structure is virtually unchanged. The house was divided into two cottages in the early 19th century, but is now back as one residence. There is a fair amount of evidence that certain north/south roads in this part of the County became in the Middle Ages pilgrims' highways to Canterbury with a number passing through

Vine Cottage, 215/217 North Street, Romford

Tadlows, Corbets Tey Road, Upminster

Crown Farm, London Road, Romford

Willows, Wennington

Upminster Court
Stable Block

174

Bury Farm, Upminster

285/287 St Mary's Lane, Upminster

Aspen Tree Cottage, Hall Lane, Upminster

Hole Farmhouse, Hole Farm Lane, Great Warley

Hulmers, Warley Street

Brick House Hotel, Warley Street

176

Brentwood on their way to the Thames. Although some of the routes still remain today as principal roads through the area a number have reverted to lanes or footpaths. One of these is a route from Warley village green down Hole Farm Lane past Cobham Hall and Franks Farm manor house and then up Clay Tye Road to the Ockendons and thence to the Thames. Hulmers and Brick House are adjacent buildings in Warley Street just north of the Southend Arterial Road. Hulmers is mid-18th century with possibly Brick House, which is now an hotel, being a little older as the 18th century façade hides a 16th century frame. Since starting this work Hole Farmhouse, Hulmers and Brick House have been transferred to Brentwood Borough, as has Wrightsbridge Road.

West Lodge, 201 Corbets Tey Road, Upminster

Romford Golf Club House

177

Harold Court

Manor Farm, North Ockendon

Harold Wood Hall, after the fire, September, 1991

# UNLISTED BUILDINGS

During my perambulating around the Borough, taking photographs of the Listed Buildings featured in the previous section, I came across other properties which, although not of Listed status, justified a mention in this work. I have selected just five buildings although I am sure that readers could identify other old properties which should justify inclusion. Space precludes a larger selection in this category.

The first two are Harold Wood Hall and Harold Court. The top photograph shows Harold Wood Hall just after a fire in September, 1991, which left the house without a roof, but structurally complete. The house can be found in Neave Close, Harold Hill, but is best viewed from the Colchester Road (A12) near Gallows Corner. The house was built in 1847 and is described as an Italianate villa on two floors. It was a private house employing a number of servants until at least the 1930s. Judge Edward Bryant lived there from 1890 to 1926. For many years now the property has been in the ownership of the local authority and following the fire it is being converted into homes for homeless families.

Harold Court, although approached from Harold Court Road, Harold Wood, is just within the Upminster parish boundary, as the house lies on the south side of the Romford/Brentwood railway line. Like Harold Wood Hall, Harold Court is also built in the Italianate style and was constructed in 1868 for W R Preston, a solicitor, farmer and land developer who undertook in 1871 to dispose of Brentwood's sewage on part of his land. He became bankrupt in 1881 and absconded and soon afterwards the house was taken over by Shoreditch children's home. It has subsequently been used as an Essex lunatic asylum (1892-1918), tuberculosis sanatorium and was sold to Essex County Council in 1960 for educational uses.

Moving into North Ockendon, mention should be made of Manor Farm which, although only built in about 1900, stands on the site of an old manor house. Manor Farm stands on the corner of Ockendon Road and Pea Lane and has a history dating back to at least the 16th century. This manor was always closely associated with North Ockendon Hall manor and was owned by that manor right up to the time when Richard Benyon was lord of the manor in the 1930s. The wrought iron gate bears the initials `R B 1865'. Manor Farm was known as the manor of Groves until the 1770s. Another name which has changed through the centuries is Ockendon Road which used to be called Cole Street.

At Havering-atte-Bower. Havering Hall was built in 1858/59 on the site of an earlier 18th century house. In 1979 it was bought by Saint Francis Hospice, opening its doors for patients in 1984. The house is approached from the top end of Broxhill Road and commands a large site extending round into North Road opposite the village green.

Romford Golf Club occupies about 100 acres of land previously part of the Gidea Hall estate. This land was sold to the club in the early 1890s with the club opening in May, 1894. The photograph of the clubhouse is dated about 1915 although it is little changed today.

Havering Hall                                                          Upminster Tithe Barn

Broadfields Farm, Pike Lane, Upminster

# ANCIENT BARNS AND OTHER MONUMENTS

Within the London Borough of Havering there are three agricultural buildings of significant importance to have been given Listed status or declared an Ancient Monument. In addition there are a number of other objects which have also been officially recorded as being of historic interest.

The most well known historic barn is the Tithe Barn in Hall Lane, Upminster, owned by the London Borough of Havering and in the care of the Hornchurch & District Historical Society and houses the Agricultural and Folk Museum. The barn is adjacent to Upminster Hall (Upminster Golf Club) and was formerly part of this manor's outbuildings. The barn is a large timber framed building with a thatched roof and clad in horizontal weatherboarding. It was built about 1450 by Waltham Abbey, who held Upminster Hall manor (see Upminster Hall). Although the building is known locally as the 'Tithe' barn there is no evidence that it was ever used to collect tithes from the villagers of Upminster as Upminster Hall manor never had that right. The right to collect tithes was held by the Rector of St Laurence Church, Upminster whose tithe barn was adjacent to the Rectory in St Mary's Lane. That barn was demolished in the 1860s.

The Hall Lane barn was first restored in 1966, when the old corrugated roof was replaced with Norfolk reeds. Following a fire in the thatch in 1973 this was replaced by the local authority and further restoration work was carried out in the 1970s, which entailed the replacing of the cladding and the base of the barn, which now has a proper concrete and brick foundation. Apart from minor repairs the roof structure remains unchanged. The museum opened on the 1st May, 1976, and is open on various weekends during the year.

The second barn of interest is at Broadfields Farm, off Pike Lane, Cranham. As can be seen from the photograph the barn has a similar shape to the Tithe Barn, although it is tile clad. This barn is also a Listed Building and, although now in public ownership, only a little work has been done on restoration and due to its rather exposed position there is danger of deterioration. The barn is 17th century.

Warren Farm Barn is situated at Warren Farm, off Whalebone Lane North, and just within the Havering borough boundary. The barn is a large red brick building with a red tiled roof and built in the 18th century. The land on which it stands is owned by the Crown Commissioners. Warren Farm stands on the site of Marks (see Marks) which was a moated mansion which stood for about 350 years and was demolished in 1808. The barn would have been an outbuilding of this old house. Restoration work has been completed on the internal timbers and part of the tiled roof.

In addition to the Tithe Barn, which is recorded as an Ancient Monument (the other barns are just Listed Buildings), there are two other pieces of land in the Borough having Ancient Monument status. These are 'The Moated Site at Dagnam Park' and the 'Roman Road across Romford Golf Course'. The moat looks more like a pond today and is a favourite fishing ground for the local community. This area of water was not the moat for

Dagnams mansion, Harold Hill which was about half a mile farther north, but the site of the moat of Cockerells the last property having stood outside the moated area (See Dagnams and Cockerells). Little can be said about the Roman road as little is known about this period of Havering's history. It is widely believed that the Roman settlement of Durolitum was probably in the Romford area although the exact location is not known. Roman remains have been found in the north eastern part of the Borough at Collier Row, Noak Hill and Harold Hill and the section of Roman road found is fairly close to these areas.

Finally in this section on non-residential monuments we must not overlook the various marker stones in and around the Borough. There are various stones that marked the boundary of the old Liberty of Havering and there are also other boundary posts and coal duty posts which have acquired Listed status. Details of these can be found at the Borough's Planning Office.

Warren Farm, Romford

# INDEX